HOW TO LOSE A MARATHON

A STARTER'S GUIDE TO
FINISHING IN 26.2 CHAPTERS | JOEL H.
COHEN ☆

ABRAMS, NEW YORK

Editor: Samantha Weiner
Designer: Devin Grosz
Production Manager: Kathleen Gaffney

Library of Congress Control Number: 2016949531

ISBN: 978-1-4197-2491-6

Printed and bound in the United States
10 9 8 7 6 5 4 3 2 1

Abrams Image books are available at special discounts when
purchased in quantity for premiums and promotions as well
as fundraising or educational use. Special editions can also
be created to specification. For details, contact specialsales@
abramsbooks.com or the address below.

ABRAMS The Art of Books
115 West 18th Street, New York, NY 10011
abramsbooks.com

Dear _____,

Great to meet you. Glad to hear you loved the book, and thank you for using the word "brilliant" so many times. As punctuation to our life-changing meeting (your words), here's my autograph:

_____

(The above pre-written inscription is just there to speed up the long line at the many book signings I'm sure to have. To speed things up further, please fill in your own name before you get to the table, where I'm probably sitting next to someone whose main job seems to be making sure I have enough bottled water. Actually, if you want, feel free to sign my name in the book, too. That would *really* speed things up.)

FOR S, R & S

***NOT* for:**
M, B, N, R and S (different R and S than above),
V, and the guy who took the parking spot I clearly
had been waiting for. (He looked like an L.)

AUTHOR'S NOTE

"A LONG RUN IS BEST DESCRIBED IN A SHORT BOOK."
—JOEL COHEN, AUTHOR OF *HOW TO LOSE A MARATHON*

There's really no purpose to this other than the fact that I've always wanted to write an "author's note." In fact, I wanted to write the note more than I wanted to be an author, but they won't let you write the note unless you churn out a book or *something* to go after it. This time I played by their rules, but next time, all I'm writing is the note. Let's see them stop me.

Anyway, this book is, if not totally accurate, accurate enough. Everything in it pretty much happened, but in many cases, events have been exaggerated or restated in a desperate attempt to make them entertaining and/or funny. I didn't change any individual names since the person I mostly disparage is myself (that should cut down on lawsuits—I say "should" because I'm unpredictable at best). I left corporate names as they were, because from what I understand, giant corporations never sue anybody.

CONTENTS

INTRODUCTION

In 2013, I lost the New York City Marathon.

I know I lost because a guy named Geoffrey Mutai won, and I have a different name than him. If that wasn't proof enough, he also finished 26,781 places in front of me.

I was disappointed to finish 26,782nd, but I was even more heartbroken to miss out on 26,781st place by less than a second. Less than a single second. The blink of an eye. I trained as long as I did, pushing myself to finish in the top 26,781, and I just missed it. It still haunts me.

It's incredible that I ran a marathon at all, since I used to be an out-of-shape slob. I was so poorly conditioned that even typing left me gasping for air. I decided to start running and began a caterpillar-like transformation into the *slightly* out-of-shape slob that ran the race.

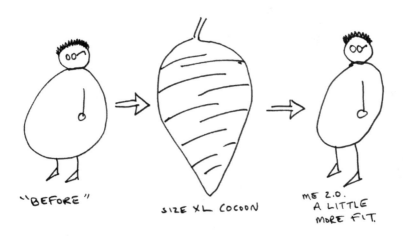

"BEFORE"

SIZE XL COCOON

ME 2.0.
A LITTLE
MORE FIT.

Even today, I can proudly say I'm still fit enough to type *several* sentences before getting winded. You may have thought these paragraph breaks were just formatting, but they're actually saving your pudgy author from a heart attack. Even now I feel my chest tightening. I need a break. This is bad. "Two returns" bad.

OK, I'm back, and surprisingly, still alive. As we both wait for my inevitable cardiac arrest, let me try to stay on point. When I made the decision to start running, I began to look for and read books about running. The second part was easy—I'm an excellent reader, reading well above my grade level. The more difficult part was finding books that informed and engaged an ignorant novice like me.

There are a lot of books about hard-core ultramarathoners and triathletes (I quickly learned I'm a uni-athlete at best), but there were none for the beginner grinder runner—the guy or girl who will probably never finish a marathon in less than four hours. The guy or girl presumably like you and me.

NOTE: I know that the above paragraph bundles you and me in the same group, and I can understand if you are insulted by the idea. If it makes you feel any better, I'm not happy being associated with me, either. Regardless, we both need to get over it. It happened. Let's move on and not make this weird.

So, much like a guy who can't find a good sandwich and then opens his own sandwich shop, or like someone who can't find the right size paperclip and then acquires an international steel conglomerate to forge them, I decided to write the book about running I wish I could have read.

Yet another stimulus for this book was to give hope to people who would like to run a marathon but think they could never do it. To all those people, let me tell you: You can.

I've observed that people are more prone to believe they can do something if they know someone who's already done it. The impossible suddenly seems possible, within reach even. I think that's why so many actors have siblings who also are actors—the crazy idea of being a working actor isn't so crazy when your brother or sister is already doing it. I suspect Stephen Baldwin saw his brother Alec acting and thought, "Hey, I can do that, too." This is why we, the public, may have a class-action suit against Alec Baldwin for unleashing Stephen Baldwin upon us.

This theory also holds true in my career. I was led to believe I could become a TV writer because my older brother was one. This is also why the public may have a class-action suit against my brother for unleashing my crappy writing on society. If you are looking for people to join the suit, count me in—you have no idea how much of my own bad writing I've had to read.

Regardless, if you are reading this and you don't know anyone who has ever run a marathon, well, now you do. Me. I did it. And trust me, if I did, you can, too.

With this book, I made an effort (and effort is something I don't usually make) to avoid writing merely about my experience for the sake of my ego. A lot of books about people doing unusual things are nothing more than thinly veiled bragging, with the author crowing, "Look what I did!" I really wanted this book to be the opposite of that. You may think that means I want it to be thickly veiled, like with a veil made out of lead, but that's entirely wrong. I can't believe that's what you thought.

What I actually meant is that instead of bragging, I'd like this book to be more a retelling of how I, a lazy lump with more chins than trophies, actually ran a marathon. From the depths of my ineptitude, I want you to find inspiration. If it's done right (and we both know it won't be), instead of saying, "Look what I did!" this book should say, "Look what I did, and now imagine how much better *you* can do!"

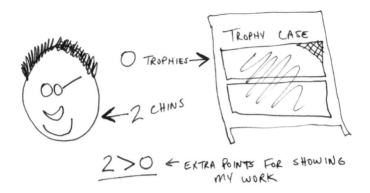

Lastly, as I detail my journey from a guy who barely finished *Marathon Man*, the movie, to a guy who barely finished a marathon, I will try to highlight relevant advice when and where I have it. Keep in mind, none of these tips come from a professional runner or a professional trainer, but maybe that's why they're worthwhile: They're the little things a complete amateur (me) saw, felt, experienced, and now feel merit passing on.

This book is *not* for anyone who has won a marathon. In fact, if I ever see Mr. Geoffrey Mutai reading it, I will rip it out of his hands and run away. I'm sure he will catch me—after all, he's Geoffrey Mutai and I'm me—but until he does, I will enjoy every one of those sweet four seconds of justice.

Enough backstory. Enough explanation. You already borrowed/ illegally downloaded/accidentally clicked the wrong button and are now stuck with this book. Whatever the reason, it's time for me to start doling out the genius and insights of the guy who finished the 2013 New York City Marathon in 26,782nd place and lost. Yes, lost.

HONEST
SELF-ANALYSIS

I'm not fast, but I am lazy.

I'd like to deal with these one at a time, since I am too lazy to deal with them both at the same time.

First, let's explore my laziness. I'm so lazy that before writing this book, I googled "how many pages does a book have to be." The answer suggested the bare minimum is forty thousand words. This book is not forty thousand words. Therefore, it may not even be a book; you may be reading a brochure, a flyer, or a long-winded fortune cookie. However, what you are holding is with certainty the product of a lazy person.

If you aren't convinced yet, let me tell you that I have an electric toothbrush, a product meant for people too lazy to move their hand in small circles for thirty seconds. I bought an electric toothbrush to avoid that torture and then, when the battery ran out, I was too lazy to reach over and place it in the small holder that recharges it. This extreme level of sloth is exactly why now, every night, I find myself moving my hand in small circles for thirty seconds. I'm so lazy I've chosen to do the "work" of brushing my teeth just so I can avoid doing the "work" of plugging in my toothbrush.

MY SPIRIT ANIMAL IS A BEACHED WHALE

I am also not fast. Not even close. Not even close to close. I'm almost the opposite of fast. (If only there was a word for the opposite of fast—it would come in so handy right now.)

I haven't always been not-fast. There was a time where I would even have described myself as "speedy." In fact, when I was younger, I was the fastest runner in my grade school class.

Now, this section is called "Honest Self-Analysis," so let me be up-front about the fact that my grade school class was made up of only six people—four boys and two girls. You might think that's a very small class until I tell you that my grade school was a Yiddish language school in Calgary, Canada. Now you're thinking, "They managed to find six people for that?!"

As fast as I was in my tiny class at the I. L. Peretz School, I couldn't keep reality at bay forever. While the list of Yiddish-speaking Canadian sprinters is long and distinguished, I was about to learn that I would not join the esteemed ranks of Gordy "Lightning" Abramowitz and the great Doug "Flash" Mendelson.

My wake-up call came when I left this little academic shtetl and entered the public school system for grade seven. There, at John Ware Junior High, I went out for the track team and returned humiliated.

It seems that when you expand your class size beyond six, and beyond the children of parents who believed Yiddish was a necessary tool for success in the twentieth century, athletic competition becomes, well, competitive.

That first track practice at John Ware gave me a chance to study the backs of my new classmates as they sped past me. I also got to see their sides as they sped past me for a second time. Then, I watched them in profile as they passed me for the third and fourth times. It was very clear—I was a slow runner, and with all this watching my peers, a bit of a stalker. At the Peretz School, I thought I was the rabbit that greyhounds chase at the dog track. At John Ware, I learned I'm more like the guy who carries a scoop and picks up after the dogs when the race is done.

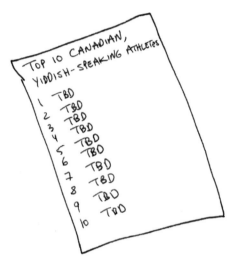

Once I came to terms with my lack of running aptitude, I began to look for other sports I could also be bad at. Luckily, I found several. Basketball—horrible! Football—below average! Jai alai—never tried it, but bet on it once in Tijuana before I realized it was fixed. Yes, I was even bad at betting on sports.

Aside from one forgettable season playing Little League Baseball, the only organized sport I played, and still play regularly, is ice hockey. When I describe this as organized I mean I play in a league that has games starting at ten thirty Sunday night and ending Monday morning. To give you a sense of the quality of play, the team I'm on started in the silver level, then dropped to the bronze level, and now the league is desperately searching for a metal less valuable than bronze so they can create a new tier worthy of our play. (My guess: It will be tin or possibly rust.)

Though I play hockey regularly, I still suck at it. I've been playing for more than forty years, and I clearly peaked the very first time I put on skates. As a proud Canadian, being a bad hockey player is a problem. Even now, in my league in Los Angeles, I try to hide that I'm Canadian so my hockey ineptitude won't reflect poorly on my homeland. In spirit, it's a very patriotic act. I don't know if anyone has ever been given the Order of Canada for denying they are Canadian, but this may merit serious consideration. Please write your local member of Parliament.

As bad as I am, I keep playing hockey because I enjoy it. I know I stink; I just like being out there, and making matters worse, I'm also a little competitive. Not the psycho competitive guy we all know and hate, but competitive enough that I try as hard as I can. The fact that I am trying to play well may come as a shock to my teammates on the Los Angeles Thunder, but it's true.

I know I'm bad at sports, yet I still love sports. I love them as much as I hate exercise. The only exercise I like to do is through sports, because I need the competition to make the physical effort interesting. That very illogical contradiction explains (or doesn't explain) where my head was at in the fall of 2012.

INSPIRATION FOR PERSPIRATION (AND EXPIRATION?)

2

In addition to suffering from an allergy to athletics, in 2012, I was also working as a writer on *The Simpsons*.

HOMER, AS DRAWN BY ME. ALSO, PROOF WHY I AM NOT AN ANIMATOR ON "THE SIMPSONS"

If you're not familiar with *The Simpsons*, *Time* magazine called it the "greatest television show of the twentieth century." I started working there almost exactly at the start of the twenty-first century, thus ensuring it would not repeat its title. If not the greatest television show, few would argue that *The Simpsons* is the most successful. As I write this, we are in the middle of producing our six hundredth episode. The show is seen all over the world and has cranked out every piece of merchandise you could ever imagine. (Unless you're imagining a Moe the Bartender PVC pipe connector. We don't have those. Yet.)

I ♡ (PVC PIPE CONNECTOR)

I was incredibly lucky to even get a job at *The Simpsons*, and I am even luckier to somehow keep my job there. I work with an amazing team of people every day on a product that is loved all over the world, just like PVC pipe connectors. My workday there pretty much consists of sitting around a table saying things I hope are funny, while assistants bring in free lunch and coffee. In those rare moments when someone isn't bringing us calories, there is also a room full of potato chips, soda, and ice cream just a few steps away.

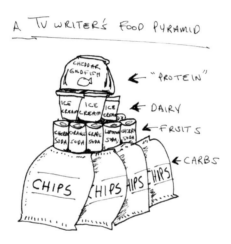

It's not like we are forced to eat sugary, delicious snacks. We can also eat salty ones. Or frozen ones. Yes, there are healthier options available, but to get to them, you have to pass the ice cream and chips, and who has the willpower to do that? The ice cream and chips are even closer to the writers' room than the bathroom is. I'm not always in the position of having to choose between the bathroom and a Creamsicle, but when I am, Creamsicles win every time.

With this setup, my workplace at *The Simpsons* is a far better environment for raising veal than raising athletes. Seeing this opportunity, greedy executives once actually placed a baby cow in the writers' room for a while. Sure, the cow was handy when we were looking for a line of dialogue for a bovine character, but other than that, it didn't work out. Things got really awkward when people ordered burgers for lunch or used the cow's milk for their coffee. You just can't have that kind of tension in the workplace.

Sitting all day, taking in high-fat foods and churning out low-quality jokes, I really didn't seem to be a candidate to run a marathon, but still, I did. Trying to understand how this happened, I examined the past with the fevered hindsight and desperation of someone trying to shore up an argument for their book. What I came up with was a lot of blame leveled at many external sources, with me ducking any myself. That's what heroes do.

Specifically, I identified several scapegoats to fault for getting me into running:

1) Every teacher I've ever had. This long line of perpetrators stubbornly taught me how to read, against my will. I was never consulted in the matter, and still, before I knew it, I had a love of reading. Oh, how I wish there was a book like this one that could have extinguished my love of reading, but there wasn't, and I consumed book after book. This literary spiral takes me to the next person I would like to blame—the author Christopher McDougall.

FROM THEN ON, IT WAS "OUR" TREE

2) Were I blissfully illiterate, I never would have read the bestseller *Born to Run* by Christopher McDougall. The book details the fascinating Tarahumara Indians of Mexico. The Tarahumara can run all day without injury, with only the simplest sandals for shoes. This basic form of running really resonated with runners who suffer from

chronic injuries and fueled the concept of barefoot running. The thesis behind barefoot running is that it employs the foot in the way it was intended to work in the human animal, and that the high-tech running shoes of today hamper that style and lead to injuries. An interesting idea, and certainly why you now see people out running in their actual bare feet or in the most minimal shoes possible. The exception to this is when you see someone in their bare feet running out of a sporting goods store carrying a pair of shoes. That is called shoplifting and is not covered in Mr. McDougall's book.

As interesting as the idea of barefoot running was, the part of *Born to Run* that really surprised me was that there are people out there who love to run. I honestly never believed people could actually *enjoy* running. Don't they know it's exercise? Accepting that running is something some people like, I, chunky and curious, was intrigued.

3) Lastly, as with any list meant to spread blame, I'd like to blame my parents, specifically, my father. My father was even less athletic than I am (hard to believe, I know, but true). He passed away right about the time I started thinking about running. Without being fully aware of it, I realize now that this reminder of our mortality made me a little more health conscious and contributed to my decision.

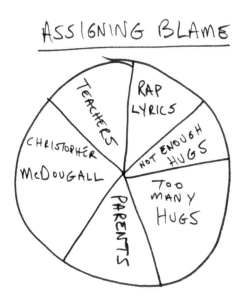

Those three forces merged just like the Allegheny, Monongahela, and Ohio Rivers merge together in Pittsburgh. An apt reference since in 2012, my physical condition was a lot like ... well, Pittsburgh. Now, before the people of Pittsburgh get insulted thinking this is a disparaging comment, let me be clear. When I compared my physical condition to Pittsburgh, I meant that, like Pittsburgh, my body is also slowly spreading out while at the same time trying to revitalize its core. I'm sure that soothes any hurt feelings. Phew.

I had thus decided I would try running. But before I could, I had a lot of procrastinating to do.

OVERTHINK AND UNDER-RUN

3

> "The will to win means nothing without the will to prepare."
> —JUMA IKANGAA, 1989 NYC MARATHON WINNER
>
> (This reminded me to prepare a will in case running kills me. I think I'll leave the Tetris game on my phone to my brother. I'm on level six, so I'm sure he'll be thrilled.)

Deciding to try running was only the first step toward running my first step. Wanting to set myself up for success, I decided to overthink everything. I wasn't great at getting started, but I was really talented at stalling. A prodigy. An Olympic-level talent. Therefore, I asked myself:

"Where to run?"

"When to run?"

"Who to run with?"

WHERE TO RUN?

There were two big options here: run outside on the street or inside on a treadmill. There may be someplace where people can run outside on treadmills or inside on streets, but thinking about both makes my head hurt, so let's stick to my reality.

When considering the idea of a treadmill, I had heard the common complaint that you buy them but never use them. This was not true in my house. We had bought a treadmill years ago, and we were using it every day to support several boxes of stuff that used to be in our garage. We had long ago forgotten what was in the boxes, but thankfully that treadmill saved them from sitting on the floor. Money well spent.

With hindsight, I now recognize there are some benefits to treadmills, aside from their potential to have boxes stacked upon them:

1) Weather: If you're running indoors, bad weather isn't a concern. I know about weather. I don't know about barometric pressure or cold fronts, but growing up in Canada, I know about bad weather. As a boy, when I would walk to school, I did everything I could to avoid the local bully. Unfortunately that was impossible, because the bully was the weather. It would blow a frozen wind in my face until I started to cry. Then it would freeze the tears right on my eyelashes. It would also make sure that somehow my tongue would get stuck to the metal of my ski jacket zipper, and finally, when I escaped inside the school, the

radical change in temperature would make my thick eyeglasses immediately fog over. Eyelashes frozen shut, mute, and blinded, I was the
Abominable Nerd. Oh, how I yearned to live someplace warm where
I could wear shorts and a T-shirt to school, where the bully was just a
troubled fat kid from a broken home.

Anyway, I know there's no way someone can risk running on snowy,
slushy, or icy roads. If you live somewhere cold and it's winter, the decision has been made for you—you're running inside.

2) Data!: If the previous description of me as a child didn't convince
you I was a nerd, I just put an exclamation point after the word "data."
Even looking at it now, I feel obliged to wedgie myself. What I mean
about data is that you will get your fill of it from a treadmill. Pace, distance, calories burned, even heart rate—all visible as you plod along.

3) TV!: You can run on a treadmill and watch TV at the same time.
Pretty sweet, right? It really makes you feel bad, thinking of those poor
rowers and skiers who have to look at boring old nature when you
are running indoors, watching something way better, like the Nature
Channel.

It's not all peaches and cream with treadmills, however. There are
some drawbacks, such as:

1) You are running indoors. As warm and "not winter" as indoors
is, running on a steady surface does not replicate the experience and
conditions you will face when you run outdoors in a race. You won't
feel wind resistance, changes in elevation, hills, dips, etc. You also
won't get practice dodging hazards like potholes or angry dogs.

Most treadmills can elevate and adjust to mirror an outdoor course, and you can hire someone's rabid dog to bite you mid-run, but it's never exactly the same.

2) Treadmills are boring. Some runners even call them "dreadmills" behind their backs. Not me—I would never say something so mean, but I also didn't stop the other runners from mocking the treadmills, which, according to my mom, makes me just as guilty. I know that while running on a treadmill you can be entertained watching TV, or if you are in a gym, you can watch the people around you slowly grow sweatier as they watch TV, but running on a treadmill is still repetitive. While running outside you have the variety of changing scenery, passing cars, other runners, and grazing Peruvian llamas (**NOTE:** This last one is only for readers in Peru, or readers whose towns have recently had a security breach at their zoo).

3) Treadmills are expensive. Most decent ones cost at least a thousand dollars, and better ones double or triple that. If that's out of your budget, that leaves only one affordable, practical option—visit a place that sells treadmills and steal a piece every time you go. After just three hundred visits, you'll be able to build your own treadmill at home for free!

If you're one of those people who are nervous about being arrested and ruining your life, you can always join a gym and use the treadmill there. Not only does joining a gym cost money, too, but to run a marathon you'll need to go on some long runs. Runs that take hours. *Hours. Of running.* My limited experience with gyms (mostly me walking by a gym entrance, eating an ice cream cone) tells me that you can't monopolize a piece of equipment for hours.

I live in Los Angeles, so the weather wasn't the issue—my frugality was. I chose to run outside. If you live somewhere colder and don't want to spend the money, I offer yet one more, foolproof solution: Start stealing the treadmill parts but do a bad enough job of it that you get arrested. In court, plead guilty to the charges, and then at your sentencing, ask the judge to send you to a prison with a "nice gym." If the judge doesn't help you with this, well, that's what the appeals process is for.

WHEN TO RUN?

Aside from weekends, it boiled down to three choices: run in the morning, run at night, or try to go for a run in the middle of the day. Let me address these out of order.

My workdays are pretty unpredictable, so trying to get out for a run midday seemed like a long shot. Even if I did, being red-faced and covered in sweat may have been a good look for my first high school dance, but it probably wasn't going to go over well with my colleagues.

Also because of work, I often don't get home until late, and I'm often exhausted from sitting around and eating all day (you really feel it in the butt and the jaws).

That left me one choice—run in the morning. I like to drive my kids to school, so it quickly became clear that if I was going to run, I had to do it early in the morning. Really early. Like wake up a rooster early. It was going to be tough. I generally stay up pretty late at night, working, watching TV, and burgling my neighbors' homes. (One of those three items isn't true. The first one. Like I'm gonna work after coming home from work, come on.)

I go to bed late and try to sleep as late as I can, but if I was going to run, things were going to have to change. Morning it would be.

WAIT, THERE'S ACTUALLY A 5 IN THE MORNING?

WHO TO RUN WITH?

I had seen people running in groups. I'd be out walking and a pack of runners would appear out of nowhere, quickly gain on me, swarm around me, and then move on, leaving me dizzy, wind-burned and in a cloud of their body odor. Through this odorous fog, I watched them go, wondering what running with a group was like.

Even if I wanted to run with others, I had no idea how to go about it. Do I try to find people who run at the same pace as me, whatever that was? Do I try to find people who like to run the same distance as me, whatever that was? I didn't know anything about how I would run, so how could I find a partner? Add to that the challenge of trying to find people I'd like to spend time with. And then, the biggest challenge of all—finding people who like spending time with me.

Regardless, I looked into finding a running partner or group and discovered the most popular ways runners come together:

Running clubs: There are thousands of running clubs, and since I live in Los Angeles, there were dozens of them near me. Choosing one would take just a little work, but the concept of even "a little work" stopped me from researching further.

Even in my permanent state of dormancy, I couldn't help but hear about what is probably the most prominent running club—the Hash House Harriers. The Harriers are very social, often offering up their slogan, "a drinking club with a running problem." The club started where and when you might expect a running club to start—in Malaysia in 1938. There and then, a group of British officers and expats began running and named their loose group after the Hash House, a club several of them lived and dined in. Today there are more than two thousand Hash House chapters around the world eager to punish both your legs and liver.

The Harriers even have their own style of running events (known as "hashes"). At these, one or more members (known as "hares") lay a trail for the pack of runners (known as "hounds") using sawdust, flour, chalk, or even toilet paper (known as "toilet paper"—they don't have a name for everything).

There are of course other running clubs that don't believe in defacing the city, and many of them also offer training programs for marathons, but I decided a club wasn't right for me. I was already in Ralph's Club (a way to save money at the supermarket), and I didn't want to spread myself too thin on the club front.

Online message boards: Yes, online message boards aren't just a great way to meet your murderer under the guise of selling a couch for four dollars. They also connect runners. On the bigger message boards like Craigslist, there are "activities" sections where people list all sorts of nonsexual, non-home-invading activities. If you are also interested in something a little more illicit than running, rest assured there's still the other 98.3 percent of the website to browse through.

Apps: Just like dating apps, there are also apps that let you find running partners. At least these apps exist at the time of this writing. Apps seem to have the same very short life span as fruit flies that drive drunk. These running partner–connecting apps work the same way dating apps like Tinder or OkCupid do, with a 20 percent less chance of contracting an STD.

Running dating club: Just think, maybe you'll find Mr. or Mrs. Right when you get together to run. Is there anything more romantic than ending your run to watch the sunrise, both of you covered in sweat and looking your worst? If you're a real romantic, pay for a violinist or mariachi band to run next to you. I considered a running dating club until my wife reminded me we are married, even presenting me with our two daughters and several tax returns to shore up her argument. I have to tell you, it was pretty convincing.

Ask at your local running store: Why not? If you can buy sweat-absorbent underwear from someone, you should be able to ask them anything.

After considering all the above, I made the decision to run on my own, lonely and ignorant. Even if by some miracle, through whatever method, I found the perfect match in pace, distance, and disposition, then what happens when we run together? Do we talk? If so, what do we talk about? The idea of using the muscles needed to carry on a conversation while also running seemed inconceivable to me.

I was completely out of excuses for why not to run. I wish I could have thought of more, but after years of finding ways to avoid unpleasantness, I had overfarmed the soil in the excuses part of my brain. I could have applied for government farm subsidies or organized a benefit concert (Excuse Aid!), but they don't exist for fictional crops. There was no way of getting out of this. It was time to run.

RUN!

4

> "Every morning in Africa, a gazelle wakes up. It knows it must outrun the fastest lion or it will be killed. Every morning in Africa, a lion wakes up. It knows it must run faster than the slowest gazelle, or it will starve. It doesn't matter whether you're the lion or a gazelle—when the sun comes up, you'd better be running."
> —CHRISTOPHER MCDOUGALL, AUTHOR OF BORN TO RUN
>
> (As mentioned earlier, I love this book. It was informative and inspiring. The above quote informed me I wouldn't last long as a lion or gazelle and inspired me not to be either. I've passed my request on to the reincarnation people and they've assured me, that in my next life, I'll come back as a shoehorn. Finally, I'll be useful.)

It was early February, and I had decided my first run was going to be the next morning. I would be waking up at a time that began with a five, and it wasn't going be pleasant for me or for my wife, who would surely also get woken up by the alarm clock. Lucky for her, as a sensitive, considerate husband, I had found a product online that would wake me without waking her—an alarm you wear on your wrist that vibrates instead of ringing. It seemed like a godsend, assuming God got into the wrist alarm business. I put it on, went to bed, and the next morning . . . it didn't work.

The product worked fine, exactly as advertised, but I found the vibration so startling and unsettling that I bolted awake, loudly screamed, "Ahhhhh! Get it off!! Get it off!" and maniacally clawed at my wrist like a bear who had just put his paw into a spring trap. Not surprisingly, my wife woke up. We decided to just go with a regular alarm from that point on.

I got dressed and stepped outside. I was amazed that I had conquered my laziness and gotten up that early, but I never considered that I had someone else's laziness to worry about—the sun's. It was almost pitch-black outside. Far be it from me to bad-mouth the sun (I gave it a two-star review on Yelp), but its only job is to stay in place and let the other planets move around it, sort of like the universe's poorly placed coffee table. The sun has held this simple job for billions of years—that's a lot of job security for a glorified traffic cone. If replacing it outright seems like a big move, why don't we at least gather some résumés? Who knows, we may find a better candidate.

For example, Neptune's always seemed pretty ambitious, and you have to respect the pressure at its core—seven megabars!

I tried to see the upside in it being dark—no one in my neighborhood would see me run. They'd just wake up and find the chalk outline and police tape around the sidewalk I died on after a futile physical effort. I had to wonder: Would they know it was me from the chalky love handles? Would my outline accurately capture the physical torture that led to my demise? I'm sure these are the same questions the residents of Pompeii asked themselves as Mount Vesuvius erupted.

I popped my earphones firmly in my ears and set out from my driveway. I put one foot in front of the other, and sure enough, I was running!

It wasn't pretty. I am not a natural runner. If I had to describe my style, I would say I looked a lot like the stumbling people do between when they have been shot and when they actually fall to the ground. The only difference was that afterward, a person who's been shot is in better physical condition than I was after running.

HOW TO LOSE A MARATHON

I kept on chugging, but it wasn't long before my lungs were aching. Then my legs joined in. From there, peer pressure (I assume) made the other parts of my body start hurting, too. In pain, huffing and puffing, I had to stop after a mile.

That first mile took me almost fifteen minutes. I probably walk a mile in twenty minutes, so this "run" wasn't much more than a walk with a good tailwind. Afterward, I was red in the face, gasping for breath, and looking for a nice spot to lie down and die. Have you ever noticed that when you're looking for a spot to lie down and die, you can never find one, but when you're out shopping for garden tools or something, you see a hundred great places to die? Just one of life's mysteries, I guess.

I went home and collapsed. The last things I remember are vultures circling overhead and a Wild West–era undertaker measuring me for a coffin. I lived, however, and I went out to run the next day. Why? Because I wanted to see how much farther I could go. Could I do a mile and a half? Maybe even two miles? My competitive nature was besting my better judgment—the same toxic combination that once led me to enter a beard-growing contest in university. I would add that I finished third in that contest, but I'm sure you already knew that. *Beard Digest* did a pretty extensive piece on me, and it was picked up nationwide by all the facial hair press.

That second run, I made it a mile and a quarter. That last quarter mile had all the grace of a train slowing to a stop after it had jumped the rails—with many of the same sound effects. But the good news was I had increased my distance! I had improved, and I felt a little bit less like dying. Is there any higher praise for something than, "I felt a little bit

less like dying?" This tiny improvement was all I needed to get up the next day for a third run. The competition against my own body was on.

I started to run every other day, seeing how much farther or faster I could get. It turned out I could do both. I began to explore my neighborhood, and later I even drove to new parts of the city to run there. I ran in parks, along the beach, and past so many mattress stores I came to understand exactly what a fair price was for a twin set.

After all this running, I started to think of myself as a runner. I soon learned I wasn't.

> "If you want to go fast, go alone. If you want to go far, go together."
> —AFRICAN PROVERB
>
> ("No matter what, don't go with Joel."
> —THE OTHER HALF OF THE PROVERB

They're out there. They look like you and me, they act like you and me, and just like you and me, they sometimes knowingly put trash in the recycling bin because there's no room left in the trash can. This is a not-so-secret community not so hidden inside ours, like a terrorist sleeper cell, except these people's only crime is getting up early and fitting into their clothes. They are . . . runners.

It was a big moment when I discovered the running community. It was an even bigger moment when I discovered I did not fit in it. Sure, there are a lot of things I don't fit in (yoga pants, the cast of *Chorus Girls*), but instead of being a runner, I realized I was merely a guy who happened to be running.

I thought of running as a hobby, as exercise even, but true runners think of it as a way of life. They're committed and addicted to running. It's their identity. There are a lot of these runners out there. This isn't just a small, maniacal fringe group, like people who still have AOL email addresses. You'll find proof of this at any newsstand, where a shocking number of magazines are dedicated to running. In fact, aside from the really important stuff like news, cats, and celebrities' beach bodies,

BIB

The little papery thing with a number on it you pin on your shirt in a race. Most races put timing chips in the bib, to track your time. **TIP:** Bring extra safety pins for your bib to smaller races. They sometimes run out.

I contend there are more running magazines than magazines about anything else.

Now that I had seen these "runners," I became adept at identifying them. I'd see the framed race bibs and finisher medals on the walls of their homes or offices. I'd notice the dirt-caked shoes in front hall closets, or the way they would take quiet moments to stretch out their hamstrings. The signs were everywhere.

If I mentioned to one of these runners that I too was starting to run, they would immediately size me up, trying to decide if I belonged among them. It was like a sorority rush party with a little less lipstick. They wanted to talk about when I ran, where I ran, how far I ran. With every answer I gave, I could see the light in their eyes dim a little more. My pace, my distances—I wasn't one of them after all.

The vast majority of runners I met were very nice, encouraging, or at the least polite, but there were some that weren't. Most of these jerks existed online, trolling and commenting, hidden behind their usernames. Cloaked in anonymity, these running purists, a.k.a. snobs, posted their race times and their accomplishments, exchanged tips, and made sure to separate themselves from people like me—people running at such a pathetic pace, they may as well be "joggers."

Still, I didn't waste a lot of time worrying about these purists and their pace-ism (a word I just made up, but am already proud of). It didn't seem like we would ever have anything to do with one another. They'd do their thing, and I would do mine—much, much slower. And then, I decided to try their thing. I decided to try a road race.

YOUR
FIRST
FIRST

6

> "To give anything less than your best is to sacrifice the gift."
> —STEVE PREFONTAINE, US RUNNER AND OLYMPIAN
>
> (This is why I always include a gift receipt. That way, instead of sacrificing anything, you can just take it back and get something you like.)

After lots of running and a little improving, I was able to run more than three miles without visions of deceased ancestors waving to me to join them. This was great because I was never a fan of family reunions anyway. Now that I could run that far, I decided to run a 5K, or a five-kilometer race. For those of you unfamiliar with the metric system, five kilometers is just over three miles. For those of you familiar with the metric system, five kilometers is five kilometers.

Aside from the Caucasians, I'd never been in an organized race before. This one was called the Santa Monica Classic and it traveled along roads parallel to the Pacific Ocean coastline. Pretty sweet. Furthermore, paying my entry fee gave me a bib, a timing chip, and my first ugly race T-shirt that I would never wear again.

Before the race, all the runners were gathered into a waiting area, lovingly and respectfully called a "corral."

I milled around in the corral, waiting for the gun to go off. (**NOTE:** that sentence was plagiarized from the sad diary of a horse with a broken leg.) When it did, the race was on, and immediately everyone started . . . walking.

That's right, they weren't running, but walking. I was passing them easily and thinking, "I'm gonna win this thing!" I then realized everyone was walking because a runner's actual race time doesn't begin until they personally step over the start line and the computer registers the chip in their race bib.

TIP: In a chip-timed race, don't push or panic to get over the starting line. There is no need to; it wastes energy, and it will also prove annoying to all the people walking ahead of you that you keep bumping into.

Once I figured out why we were walking, I embraced it. I started walking, too, and if I may brag a bit, I was keeping pace with some

CORRAL

Where runners wait before a race. In big races, there are many corrals, with runners segregated by expected finish time/speed. The faster runners go out first; the me-type runners go out last.

WAVES

In really big races, there are different waves, each made up of multiple corrals, sometimes broken down even further into different color groups to really keep things moving. Waves are released every twenty minutes or so—the formula for a successful marathon or very unsuccessful wave pool.

CHIP TIME

1) What I scream out every time I open a bag of potato chips. 2) Your race time as measured from the electronic chip in your bib or sneaker. The chip times you from the moment you step over the start line to the moment you step over the finish line. Longer races have other time strips to record your time at intervals along the way.

CLOCK TIME

The race time as measured from the starting pistol/horn/cannon to the moment you cross the finish line. If you are at the back of a crowded start or in a later corral or wave, the clock time when you finish will be very different from your chip time. In people's photos at the finish line, the clock above their heads makes them look a lot slower than they are. In my finishing photo, it was my glacial pace, the darkness, and the workmen taking the course down that made me look slow.

KICK

The final push runners give at the end of the race. Sadists, be aware there's no actual kicking involved. I'm not sure what the repercussions would be for kicking other runners, but I suspect it is frowned upon. Maybe ask your local race organizer?

pretty fit people around me. Eventually though, we stepped over the starting line; they broke into a run, and I broke into . . . whatever I did.

As I settled into my jog, I became less nervous and more excited. Pretty soon, I came across an aid station and a volunteer handed me a cup of water. I drank it and then, following the lead of the other runners, I just threw the empty cup on the ground. As a burgeoning runner, water drinker, and litterbug, this was awesome!

I continued on, enjoying being a part of this bouncing, surging mass of humanity cruising down the street. Before I knew it, the finish line was just ahead. I picked up the pace a little and charged across the line.

As I crossed the finish, I was surprised to realize I felt pretty good. I felt even better when I saw my time. I had run the 3.1 miles in 28:56 (28 minutes and 56 seconds), and what's more, I had come in 267th out of a field of 945. I had beaten almost seven hundred legitimate runners! I chose to focus on that rather than the 266 people who beat me, including some moms who ran pushing baby strollers. In my defense, the kids in those strollers were small, light, and aerodynamic, giving the moms pushing them an unfair advantage. Either way, for a first race, this was encouraging and even fun.

That race also gave me something else—a pace. Doing the math, by which I mean reading the math off the race website, I saw I had run at a pace of roughly nine minutes per mile. Nine minutes a mile. My speed had been officially measured. This was a blessing and a curse, because now that I had a pace to beat, I was even more hooked. I had to run faster.

WHILE RUNNING, I'VE BEEN PASSED BY!

OTHER RUNNERS

TUMBLEWEEDS

BABIES IN STROLLERS

BABIES OUT OF STROLLERS

NOTE: I never ran faster. Never. Even though I spent a lot of time trying to. This futile and wasted effort made me hate the concept of time, and it explains why I am still not speaking to my watch. No, not even on the holidays.

TRUE CONFESSIONS: WHY I DID IT

7

> "Pain is inevitable. Suffering is optional."
> —HARUKI MURAKAMI, AUTHOR OF *WHAT I TALK ABOUT WHEN I TALK ABOUT RUNNING*
>
> (Interestingly, "Pain is inevitable. Suffering is optional" is also one of the reviews this book has received.)

While I never ran faster than I did in the 5K, I kept pushing myself (far more socially acceptable than pushing others; I learned that the hard way). Through all this I did manage to increase my distance. I was actually seeing improvement. I never knew people could improve at sports—this was mind-blowing! Running every other day, I also started to notice my fitness improve, and I even lost some weight. Good things were happening.

As positive as the mood seems, let's stop so I can state something important. So important, it needs to stand on its own, with no other words around it:

I'VE NEVER ENJOYED RUNNING.

Nope. Never. Not once. Not even half of once. Not even two times half of once.

I enjoyed the quiet of the early morning. I enjoyed seeing myself improve. I enjoyed getting more fit, but I never enjoyed the actual motion of swinging one hairy leg in front of the other. Never. I know people do, the Tarahumara Indians for instance, but not me.

Where was this "runner's euphoria" I had read about? Where were all the endorphins that were supposed to be flooding into my brain? I was looking for the oft-mentioned "runner's high," but it turned out I had been sold a bag of runner's oregano.

The thing that kept me running was the one thing about it that I did really like, a lot, and that was *having* run. I loved the feeling of being done, of having done something—a feeling of accomplishment. Yes, instead of a runner's high, my rush came from what can only be called an "accomplisher's high." The same pleasant sensation I would get from other things in my life, like getting my car washed, or cleaning up my email inbox. I was hooked on the satisfaction of achieving a goal, no matter how small. Researchers have studied this phenomenon and have classified people like me as "dweebs." I assume that's a Latin word. I'll have to look it up.

The way I feel about running is very similar to the way I feel about writing; I hate it when I'm doing it, but I like seeing what I've done, even if it's garbage. And if you have made it this far into the book, I think you can guess it's almost always garbage.

Still, this book is a merger of writing and running—the two things I hate doing—and still I'm doing it. I'm pushing past my hatred and fears, all for you, the reader. The takeaway from this is: I'm a hero. Overcoming obstacles, facing challenges—an absolute hero.

Like every other hero, it won't be long before my selfless act is commemorated with a statue. I've been giving some thought to what pose my statue should have. Should it be me writing? Me running? Maybe me running with a laptop under my arm? Perhaps it should be me typing while someone drapes a medal over my neck? I guess in the end, I'll just go with whatever is hardest for pigeons to crap on.

LET'S TAKE THIS TO THE NEXT ILLOGICAL LEVEL

8

> "The difference between the mile and the marathon is the difference between burning your fingers with a match and being slowly roasted over hot coals."
> —HAL HIGDON, RUNNING WRITER AND COACH
>
> (Hal, I hope you didn't do any research to come up with this quote. If you did, please tell me you're getting the help you need. We're worried about you.)

Four months after that February morning when I first staggered down my driveway, I could, if I went slowly, run ten miles. When you've gone from zero to one, and from one to one and a half, and then three, and then five, and then ten, you start to wonder how much farther you can go. That exact type of idiotic thinking is what leads people to set the world record for most eggs crushed with their head in one minute (eighty, by the way) and led me to wonder if I could finish a marathon. I decided I would try and find out.

I knew very little about marathons, starting with even the most basic piece of information—the distance. It turns out a marathon is 26.2 miles, and both the name and distance come from the Greek legend of Philippides. According to the legend, Philippides was a messenger who, in approximately 490 BCE, ran from the city of Marathon (hence the name) to Athens to announce that the Persians had been defeated in battle. There's some debate about exactly what happened, including which roads he took and the distance, but in the most popular version of the legend, Philippides ran the entire way, burst into the Athenian assembly, announced excitedly, "We have won," and then collapsed and died. An inspirational story with a real bummer of an ending.

Let's take a short break here to consider the fact that the man who ran the first marathon died. Died. DEAD died. The man shouldn't be a legend, but a cautionary tale! It's like celebrating a guy who tried sleeping on a pillowcase full of cobras. Did that actually happen? Was there a real guy who tried this? No one knows, because if there was, he died! OK, I'm calming myself down now. I'm taking deep breaths, I'm listening to ocean sounds, and . . . I'm fine. Let's continue.

The race we now call a "marathon" was first run in 1896 at the first "modern" Olympics in Athens. The distance of that race was roughly twenty-five miles. At the 1908 London Olympics, the distance was lengthened to 26.2 miles (or 42.195 kilometers) so the runners could

NOT-GREAT MOMENTS IN SPORTS!

Philippides ran the first-ever marathon and died as soon as he finished. Congratulations + Condolences.

Philippides lived. ran. died.

finish in front of the Royal Box. There you have it—history made because the British monarchy didn't feel like turning their heads a little bit.

Philippides was clearly a trendsetter. Not only did he invent the marathon, but I think he also came up with the Macarena, casual Fridays in the workplace, and turning right at red lights. Nowadays, marathons are run everywhere. In 2015, there were more than 1,100 different marathons in the United States alone, with many, many more around the world. There was even one in Disney World. I mention this one separately because I'm not sure if "Disney World" is a part of our world (known as "Earth" to its friends) or if it exists as another world altogether.

I discovered that in addition to the traditional options for pushing my body through 26.2 miles, there were also a variety of choices if I wanted to add a little fun and/or death into the mix. Races like these:

The Disney World Marathon: If you're interested, the Disney World Marathon takes runners through four Disney parks (Disney World, Epcot, Disney's Animal Kingdom, and Disney's Hollywood Studios) for a two-hundred-dollar entry fee. This is a miracle since, as you know if you've ever visited a Disney park, it's impossible to walk through even one of them without spending two hundred dollars just on lunch. I decided to skip Disney as an option and keep searching.

The Great Wall Marathon: Our North American modesty only lets us call our walls "OK" or "sufficient," but in boastful China they aren't shy about labeling their wall "great." Looking past that, this marathon travels through Chinese villages and has six kilometers of running on the wall itself. The whole route demands that you climb 5,164 steps and finish in less than eight hours. That's a lot of stairs in not a lot of time. Knowing I get tired just pushing the button on an elevator, I kept looking.

Safaricom Marathon: The "com" part of the race name makes you think of a safe, serene, jungle-themed website, maybe even with a good-natured hyena in the help section that chuckles when you ask a question. Sadly, that's not what this is. Instead of focusing on the "com" part of the title, the emphasis should be on "safari," but even that is underplaying it. This marathon is run in a wildlife conservatory in Kenya, and the race literature warns runners they need to be aware of the risk of both sunstroke and animal attack. Yes, animal attack. Runners can take some solace knowing the course is patrolled by armed guards presumably ready to shoot a charging lion or the hot sun beaming down on them. Pass.

I WAS ONCE PASSED BY A GLACIER

Polar Circle Marathon: Run in Greenland, where the temperatures in this race can drop to as low as minus fifteen degrees Celsius. Runners pass by glaciers, across an arctic desert, and through the habitats of musk oxen and arctic foxes. Organizers remind runners to stay on the course with the following gentle warning: "Because of the danger of falling into a crevasse, it is strictly forbidden to leave the marked route on the ice sheet." If you weren't scared off by the temperature or the musk oxen, that last tidbit may just break you. It broke me.

Marathon du Médoc: This marathon snakes through the French countryside, passing fifty different chateaus, thirty vineyards, and more importantly, twenty-three wine tasting stations that also hand out

baguettes with cheese and ham. I imagine if I ever finished, I'd receive a medal, a T-shirt, and a diagnosis of gout. Next.

Burro Days World Championship Pack Burro Race: This race in Fairplay, Colorado, is a little different, and not just because they use the word "burro" twice in the name. As a huge fan of burros, donkeys, mules, and

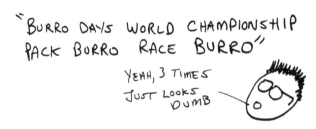

asses, I was of course intrigued. Then I learned the race is twenty-nine miles long, with a four-thousand-foot ascent, and, uh, I feel like I'm forgetting something. Oh yeah, now I remember. You have to run leading a burro carrying fifteen kilograms (thirty-three pounds) of mining gear!

There's a lot about this I don't like, but none more than thinking that these burros spend all year looking forward to "Burro Days," and then, instead of being celebrated, they have to run this race. If you're reading this and you know about or belong to a burro union, please file a grievance.

The Everest Marathon: If you're like me, you immediately thought this was a marathon sponsored by Everest, the Florida-based institution that teaches things like "medical insurance billing and coding," but it turns out, there's also a huge mountain named Everest. It sprawls from Nepal to Tibet, it's almost thirty thousand feet high, and you can run a marathon on it. Specifically, you can run a marathon down it. If you are a few steps ahead of me (and anyone I have ever run with), you'll realize that before you can run down it, first you'll need to get up it. That's right, before you can run this marathon, you need to spend fifteen days climbing up to the base camp you will start from. It's not often that getting to the starting line is worse than getting to the finish line, but here it is.

The North American Wife Carrying Championship: Not even a marathon, but a chance to race over obstacles with my wife physically on my back. I haven't discussed the idea of this with my wife, but even if she had a problem with it, I'm sure she would be appeased knowing the winners take home, among other things, the wife's weight in beer. This prize puts husbands in the difficult position of first wishing their wives weighed less and then later wishing they weighed more.

With so many race choices available, I approached the problem the way I do any big life decision. First, I excluded anything involving burros, wine, or Disney characters. Next, I eliminated anything dangerous, like steps, extreme temperatures, animal attack, or the anger of a poorly carried wife. That left me with just the boring, traditional marathons.

I could have run the Los Angeles Marathon, but I decided if I was going to have this adventure, I wanted it to be somewhere different, somewhere iconic. Almost every city has a marathon, but major cities have major marathons. The biggest six are known as the World Marathon Majors. They are:

London Marathon: Not just a chance to run through an amazing city, this marathon also holds the world record as the largest annual fund-raising event in the world. In 2002, a runner named Lloyd Scott raised money by running in a diving suit that weighed 110 pounds. He finished in a little more than five days, setting the record for the slowest London Marathon time. Out of respect for Mr. Lloyd, I passed on this race, not wanting to threaten his record with my sure to be pathetic performance.

Berlin Marathon: This race, sponsored by BMW, offers a flat course in the cool autumn weather. Unfortunately, it takes place in September when I'm busy losing money by betting on NFL games.

Tokyo Marathon: I love Tokyo. The food, the people, the culture. I wouldn't feel comfortable defacing such a beautiful city with my sweat and failure.

Chicago Marathon: This race was very appealing because it both starts and finishes in Grant Park, a course layout known as a "loop." For runners as slow as me, the Chicago loop course meant I would be able to watch the other runners finish as I was still getting started. That would give me a huge rush of motivation, followed by an even bigger surge of depression as I realized I had just been lapped by forty-seven thousand people.

Boston Marathon: The Boston Marathon is unique in that to gain entry you either need to join a charity team (more on this later) or you have to qualify to enter. To qualify, you need to have run a "good" time in another marathon. The qualifying times are fast. In 2018, for a male between forty-five and forty-nine, you have to have finished a marathon in less than 3:25. The highest age group they list is eighty and older; to qualify, you still have to have run in less than 4:55. Unless I put some rockets on my shoes or bought a fake ID that said I'm eighty-one, Boston wasn't an option for me.

That brought me to the last of the big races, to the largest marathon in the world, and in my mind, the most iconic:

The New York City Marathon. I looked and looked for reasons not to choose this one but couldn't find any. They don't ask for a qualifying time. It takes place in November when I would have already lost all my NFL betting money. No one has ever run it in a diving suit, it's a point-to-point course, and New York is generally considered to be filthy, so a little more sweat and failure wouldn't be a problem. With no reason not to run it, this was the marathon for me. Decision made.

I would run the New York City Marathon.

LOOP COURSE

The finish line is in the same place as the starting line, hence you run a 26.2-mile loop.

POINT-TO-POINT COURSE

The finish line is somewhere different than the start, hence you run from one point to the other.

COMMIT YOURSELF TO AN INSTITUTION

9

> "If you want to run, run a mile. If you want to experience a different life, run a marathon."
> —EMIL ZÁTOPEK, CZECH RUNNER AND THREE-TIME OLYMPIC GOLD MEDALIST
> (Or go to jail, live in the woods, marry a Kardashian—a few other, easier ways to experience a different life.)

I knew all the things the New York City Marathon didn't have (qualifying times, cleanliness, etc.), but I knew very little about what it did offer. Luckily, the Internet did—it's so smart! It told me that the race started in 1970 with only 127 entrants. Nowadays, more than fifty thousand runners take off every year on the first Sunday in November and travel through each of the city's five boroughs, ending in Central Park. According to the Internet, the marathon apparently also wants me to get in touch with some of my old high school classmates—unless that's just an ad that popped up on the screen. Still, I probably should. Ignoring an ad would be rude.

> **NYC seeks MAF** (Middle-Aged Fatso) for long, punishing run in November. Water and sports drink offered in exchange for sweat, effort and three years off your life span. Must enjoy personal chafing and straggling behind.

As I looked into entering the marathon, I found that it was already sold out. Apparently I wasn't the only one who had heard of this world-famous thing. The fact that it was sold out may seem obvious to you, but you have the advantage of not being stupid.

I began researching and found out that the race is so popular, to gain entrance, you have to win a lottery. Statistics show the chance of winning entry through that lottery is about 15 percent. Unlike most lotteries, however, most winners of this one don't immediately buy gold-plated Jet Skis and end up bankrupt within three years.

There are also other non-lottery ways to get into the race. One is to run a certain number of smaller races for the New York Road Runners, the group that organizes the marathon. Sadly, my one Santa Monica race did not help me in this regard. Like Boston, you can also qualify with an exceptional time in a previous race. Again, shockingly, my leisurely stumble through Santa Monica didn't help me here either. A third way is to have lost the lottery three years in a row. Although I excel at losing, this wouldn't work for me, either; I wanted to run right away. There was, luckily, one last way to gain precious entry—join a charity team.

The way a charity entrance works is the runner commits to raising a certain amount of money for the charity, and in return, they give you a guaranteed place in the race. It's the sort of selfish altruism that lets people underpay for donated luxury vacations at their kids' school fund-raiser and feel good about themselves. I'm not judging. I've done this very thing before, and I will do it again. The savings on vacations alone are almost enough reason to have kids.

Struck with a sudden desire to be charitable, I began perusing the various teams and how much they each needed in the way of a fund-raising commitment. There were many worthwhile causes, but I'm embarrassed to say I sought out the ones that asked for the lowest amount. My laziness isn't just restricted to running, but also to fund-raising. It's even worse than that: I decided I wasn't actually going to be doing any fund-raising. No, I was looking for the charity team with the lowest amount because I decided I would just pay that amount. Fat, lazy, cheap: I have just achieved the undesirable trait hat trick.

Reading the above, you may hate me. My response to that is, "What took so long?" Before that hate turns into pure repulsion, let me explain. Every marathon has these admissions reserved for charities, and it's a good thing—the New York City Marathon raises over 25 million dollars a year for various causes. For me, however, the idea of asking people to donate to a charity I chose so I can do something I wanted to do didn't sit well (and sitting is something I normally excel at). I would be asking people to donate, acting selfless, when really my motivation was selfish. I could afford to make the donation myself, so I did.

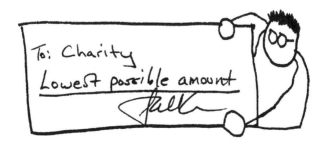

HOW TO LOSE A MARATHON

I know not everyone can afford to do this, and to those who do ask friends and family to support a cause and their race, best of luck—I pass no judgment. I state the above to inform you about my choice, and to confirm that not only am I an amazing physical specimen, but also an amazingly moral one. Maybe we can get a halo put on my statue? Two halos? OK, three, but that's it, because any more and it's going to start to look silly.

Wallet open and ready to pay, I faced yet another decision: Which of the least expensive charities should I donate to? I scrolled through my options. They all sounded like great and worthy causes, but ultimately I became a member of the team running for a charity called Shoe4Africa.

I assume you have never heard of them. I know I hadn't. Shoe4Africa, founded by a former elite runner and a fascinating guy named Toby Tanser, works to improve the life of impoverished people in Africa. Reading about Toby and the work they were doing, I was sold (especially at this discounted price!). If you want to know more about what they do, go to their website, shoe4africa.org. It's worth checking out just to read Toby's story and the consequent origin of the charity's name. As a teaser, the story involves a machete—as, I assume, all the names of charities do.

I entered my credit card information, clicked the "submit" button, and just like that, I was signed up to run the New York City Marathon. 26.2 miles. That's when the first doubts crept in. Run a marathon? Me? 26.2 miles! Me? What was I thinking?

I didn't try to get out of it, however, mostly because I didn't think I would be able to get a refund. Not getting a refund has, I am sure, been the inspiration for many amazing athletic feats. I am told Jesse Owens won his 1936 Olympic gold medals because when he phoned to cancel his trip to Berlin, the airline kept him on hold so long he got frustrated and decided it was easier just to go.

GREAT UNTRUE MOMENTS IN SPORTS HISTORY!

It looked like I was actually doing this. I had signed up to run a marathon and was on a team I hadn't disappointed yet. Both were uncharted territory.

WORK OUT
YOUR WALLET

10

> "A poor workman blames his tools."
> —PROVERB
>
> (The "tools" for running are expensive and can make you poor. Just a heads up.)

Now that I had committed myself to running the marathon, I had to get serious. A life of watching sports and the commercials that interrupt them has taught me that performance is tied to equipment. I foolishly thought running was different. Part of its beauty is that it involves almost no equipment—as stated earlier, even shoes are optional. This low cost is, I suspect, a part of the reason the best long-distance runners in the world come from "developing" countries. By the way, the term "developing countries" makes me imagine foreign economies as something that might be discussed in health class. Even now, I'm imagining a prepubescent Namibia, a blossoming Belarus, and a buxom Germany, holding its shoes in its hands on a "walk of shame" home after a night partying with the United States. If reading that made you uncomfortable, relax in knowing that this soft-core economic analogy is as erotic as this book gets.

Truth is, running a marathon does require some equipment, and shoes are just the start of it. Many of the items I am going to introduce I learned about only after I ran some more and was then able to more accurately evaluate them for their worth. Instead of making you learn the way I did, like a male, Jewish Mother Teresa I've chosen to tend to those poor in knowledge and offer my insights on what you need and what you don't:

Shoes: Thinking about the shoes I would train and run in, I contemplated the Tarahumara Indians and their basic sandals. I knew this wasn't for me. I worried about damaging my feet and them not being at their peak beauty when the coroner put the toe tag on my corpse after the marathon. So after talking to a doctor, some other runners, and of course my local clergy, I made the bold decision to run in ... shoes! (*Dramatic music goes here, then we cut to a commercial.*)

NOTE: I've just been told that this book will have neither a soundtrack nor commercials. You can imagine my embarrassment.

Having made the radical decision to wear shoes, I wandered into my local running store. There I was faced with yet another decision—which shoes should I buy? I was assaulted with choices of brand, fit, cushioning, and style. Seeing the hundreds of shoes around me, I realized the only thing I could be sure of was that whichever shoes I bought, they would be incredibly ugly.

For some reason, over the last few years, running shoes have become fluorescent and garishly colored, seemingly designed by the same people that make bright orange vests for highway workers. These shoes consequently look like what you'd end up with if you fed parrots a steady diet of light sticks and then let Jackson Pollock blow them up. In case you need a visual image, I encourage you to look up the Asics Gel Noosa Tri 10 GSD. If you think the name is a lot to handle, check out the shoes themselves; they are the physical manifestation of what would happen if street graffiti took LSD.

GOSSIP IN THE WORLD OF SHOES

In light of the way modern running shoes look, my advice is to just ignore appearances (the same advice I offered to girls when I asked them out on dates). If anyone laughs, explain there are other factors to consider (also advice I offered to potential dates). The shoes I've run in prove that I put my foot where my mouth is. I've headed out the door in shoes that were candy apple red, green, blue, and even a bright yellow pair that I'm sure carried some level of radiation.

When it comes to choosing the best ugly shoe for you, you need to understand *pronation* and *supination*. No, these are not rival street

PRONATION

Simply, and dumbly, put, pronation is the inward roll of the foot. As an aside, I've heard that an inward foot roll is a cannibal's favorite type of sushi. I suggest a pause here so you can recover from that joke. Take as long as you need; I need a minute myself.

SUPINATION

The outward roll of the foot. No joke here; I'm talking to a grief counselor, still trying to get over the last one.

gangs; even worse, they are rival movements of the foot when running.

At the store, a helpful sales clerk went right to work trying to determine how my foot rolls when running. She had me climb on a mini-treadmill and watched as I ran on it in my stocking feet. I began lumbering along, and mid-run I realized this is probably as close as I'll ever get to exotic dancing. The only exception would be if I were invited to perform at an all-blind bachelorette party. If that ever happens, fair warning to the blind bride and her maids of honor: Even if it sounds like I'm dancing (in my imaginary anticipation of this event, I've already chosen Def Leppard's "Pour Some Sugar on Me" as my song), I'm really just gonna be sitting in a chair. Even still, tips are appreciated.

After watching me run for a little while, the clerk declared I was a pronator, suggesting that I needed a shoe with some stability control. We found one that was affordable, kept my foot in place, and was a little more muted in color than a road flare.

I had shoes. I was set. Or was I? No, I wasn't. (I'm pretty good at answering my own rhetorical questions. Or am I? I am.)

Shirts: I am not a fashion plate. In my regular life, I wear almost the same thing every day, usually in some depressing shade of blue or gray. I don't like shopping and would happily vote for any law mandating that we all have to wear identical coveralls every day, like in a science fiction movie or air conditioning repair school. Be forewarned, if this inspires you to write a science fiction movie set in an air conditioning repair school, I've already written it. It's called *It Came From Outer Space Heater* and was rejected by everyone everywhere.

WICKING

As defined by everythingcloth.com (a far better resource than completely-ignorantaboutcloth.com), wicking is "the transfer of moisture from one area to another."

A wicking shirt therefore is one that removes moisture, in this case sweat, away from the body. Run in a wicking shirt and you will remain dry and cut down on the friction that comes from a wet shirt bouncing against your body. Wear a cotton shirt and you'll be both soaked and possibly sore. If you doubt this, go to possiblysore.com, a website that doesn't exist.

I will consequently leave all fashion choices up to you and offer only one bit of guidance. Pursue wicking. (Don't pursue Wiccans and wicker, for obvious and less obvious reasons, respectively.)

Sweats/shorts: Again, I will stay away from fashion advice and only encourage you to choose something that will keep you dry and cut down on friction. Experience (as you will read later) has taught me that friction below the body's equator can cause many bad things. I also suggest wearing something with a pocket that closes with a zipper. A place to keep your car keys, money, pepper spray, and if you think there's a reason for it, a small ruby you can trade with border guards to bribe your way across any border.

A running app: As I ran more, I wanted to keep track of "how far" and "how fast," and the best way to do that was with an app on my phone. The app chronicled the details of each individual run and also served as a record of all my runs. In quiet, nerdy, yet narcissistic moments, I would look back to see how I'd progressed over time. It was like a report card that, for once, I didn't have to forge my parents' signatures on! Annoying, since I had been forging their signatures on scrap paper for years, keeping my skills sharp.

There are many different running apps, and I would mention the name of the specific one I used, but why promote them unless they pay me? That's right, I'm holding the brand name hostage until this company meets the following demands:

1) Ten thousand dollars
2) A cheese named after me (NOT a goat cheese)
3) My face on the tails of Hawaiian Airline planes instead
of the woman currently featured there

Three simple things. It's just that easy, Runkeeper. Meet my demands, or no one will ever know your . . . Damn.

OK, the app I used is called Runkeeper. You got it out of me. Executives at Runkeeper: Recognizing that now I have less leverage, I have lowered my demands. I will settle for just the cheese. Even goat cheese. Or just a goat, and I'll take it from there.

My verdict: Get an app. Most of them are free, with an optional upgrade, but even with the free versions, having one is immensely helpful during and between runs.

Compression socks: The rare product sold to both runners and senior citizens, compression socks increase blood flow by compressing the veins. Runners seeking extra circulation use them while they run or to recover afterward. Old people, I assume, use them for a little extra "edge" at the bingo game. If you're considering compression socks, be advised that they cover your entire shin and calf, making your legs resemble those of a Catholic schoolgirl.

My verdict: I chose to not buy compression socks and to let my veins fend for themselves. I mean, what have my veins ever done for me?

GPS watch: You ask, "A watch? Why do I need a watch if I just got an app like you suggested? How can you be so fickle? Plus, what's up with your hair? Is that a haircut or a series of foiled knife attacks?"

OK, I'm going to stop your imaginary questions right there before I imagine you saying something that really hurts my feelings.

Yes, I know I recommended you get an app, but as you run longer distances, your phone won't last through the whole run because the app will drain the battery. You could also avoid this problem by plugging your phone into a crazily long extension cord, but that's expensive, cumbersome, and ridiculous. That's where the GPS watch comes in.

Not only will the watch tell you your pace and total distance, but after your run, you can sync the data back to your running app. If this sounds at all complicated, remember that I have the technological skills of a newborn baby, and I did it.

My verdict: Get the watch (yes, and the app). When choosing a watch, make sure it displays all the things you want to track (for me it was pace and distance) at the same time. Once I figured out how to set the display, I never messed with the watch again. I have no idea if it even tells time.

Heart monitor: Some GPS watches have these built in, or there are separate ones you can buy. Regardless, all of these heart monitors do the same thing, which is to, uh, monitor your heart. In my nonmedical, uninformed opinion, who cares what your heart rate is? You'll definitely know if there's a problem—the paramedics in the ambulance will tell you.

My verdict: Pass.

Aerodynamic sunglasses: Why should my sunglasses have an easier time than me?

My verdict: Pass.

Blister resistant socks: Sweaty feet cause blisters. That is not only a great pickup line, but also the truth. Every running gear company has thus manufactured socks that absorb sweat (yet another reason you should be glad you aren't a sock). I ran in the same cheap socks I walk, live, and go bowling in and never had a problem with blisters. All sorts of other things happened to my feet, as you will read later on (maybe the worst teaser ever?), but I don't think upgrading your socks is worth it.

My verdict: Try running in your normal socks first.

Kinesiology tape: You probably didn't know the name of this stuff but have seen it stuck onto the legs of various athletes as if they were gift-wrapped by a five-year-old. One of the companies selling this tape offers the unbiased description that it helps "change muscle tone, move lymphatic fluids, correct movement patterns, and improve posture."

My verdict: Again, pass. To be honest, I never tried tape, but I also never felt the need to. For me, the only benefit of covering myself in tape would be to hold my body together like the worn, battered suitcase full of organs it is.

The bottom line: Buy good shoes, good shirts, and good shorts. Get an app and eventually you'll want/need to get a watch. Skip the other garbage. You don't need it, and you've already wasted enough money buying this book.

TRAIN

11

> "The long run puts the TIGER in the cat."
> —BILL SQUIRES, RUNNING COACH AND AUTHOR
>
> "Proximity puts the cat IN the tiger."
> —MY RESPONSE

I suppose I could have hired a coach to train me. I also could have joined a local running group that offers specific training programs for marathons. Problem is, both of those involved interacting with other people, and who wants that? No, instead I planned to train in dark, sweaty solitude, the same way I came to master the 1980s Mattel Intellivision game *Bump 'n' Jump*. Sadly, Intellivision neither had a training program nor existed in 2013, so instead I relied on my aforementioned running app. It not only tracked my runs but also had a marathon-training program that specified exactly what I had to do each day.

The program laid out three smaller runs Monday to Friday, each ranging from three to six miles, and then a long run on Saturday. Trust me, I am as shocked as you are that six miles is considered a "smaller" run. If for some reason you aren't shocked, then admittedly I am more shocked than you are. If you are really shocked, to the point that you have read the first sentence of this paragraph over and over, shaking your head and saying "Gosh!" each time, then I am less shocked than you are.

I followed the program religiously. (If I had to specify a religion, I would say Baha'i.) After finishing each specified run, a little icon on the program would turn from an unhappy yellow face to a green check-mark. Making that little yellow face happy somehow made me happy. Yes, I know this is pathetic and desperate, but it's also the truth.

Getting into the program a little more specifically, there were a few types of runs that weren't just defined by distance. These asked for different types of running. They were:

Tempo runs: This does not mean running faster than a Ford Tempo, even if you easily can. A tempo run is a fast run sandwiched between a slower warm-up run and a slower cool-down run. If we are really committing to the sandwich analogy, we'd slowly heat one piece

of bread and slowly cool the other, while the meat in between stays at a consistently high temperature. It sounds like a horrible sandwich, which is why I am dropping that analogy.

Fartleks: There's no denying that this term has the word "fart" in it. Normally, this would prove incredibly tempting for me to joke about. I'm already conjuring up scenarios where Superman's archvillain Lex Luthor ate spicy food, but I will resist that urge and try to stay professional. I can't promise I'm going to make it, but please appreciate the intent and the effort.

Fartlek literally means "speed play" in Swedish, although knowing that won't help you much unless you are in Stockholm looking for live theater performed by actors on amphetamines.

Fartlek training is simply mixing fast running with slower running in the same training session, often in an unstructured way. For example, you may decide, on the spot, to sprint to a lamppost and then jog to a water fountain. Observers of this may think you are crazy. Stop and explain to them this is just fartlek training, and then they will be sure you are crazy.

Interval runs: Intervals are defined as short, intense runs separated by some recovery time. The pace is often set so fast that it's hard to maintain it for much longer than the interval. The difference between interval runs and fartleks is that intervals are structured in exact times or distances, while fartlek training is more improvised.

2 TYPES OF SPLITS AND NEITHER IS A BANANA SPLIT. REALLY?

Splits: The term "split" can refer to two different things. The first is the time it takes to run a mile. After a run, you can look at your split times on your app and compare how you ran one mile against another. The second definition is the time it takes to run half a race. There are, of course, all sorts of other definitions that have nothing to do with running. There are also all sorts of other words that have nothing to do with running, but now I'm just babbling.

Negative splits: This refers to running the second half of something faster than the first. I was told it is very hard to negative split a marathon. That proved true, as did the idea of positive splitting a marathon. Basically, anything about running a marathon proved hard and true.

Easy run: No, this is not a run that the gossips in town have pegged as "easy" because of its flirtatious nature. Instead, this is the term for a run done at a light, conversational pace. I dream of a day when I get fast enough to have a slower gear I could call conversational. Right now, an easy run for me is called "lying down."

Recovery run: A short, slow run the day after a longer, harder run. This supposedly teaches the body how to work even in a fatigued state (think West Virginia). This education is meant to come in handy around mile eighteen of a marathon, when you're tired and still have over eight miles to go.

Rest day: Taking a day off lets your muscles recover a little bit. While I missed some of the prescribed training runs, I'm proud to say I never missed a rest day.

With that basic knowledge of the different types of training, I thought long and hard about the value of detailing all my training runs (both lies—I thought about it short and easy). Ultimately, and lazily, I decided to list them all in an appendix. If so inclined, check it out to compare yourself to me, and it will leave you feeling better about yourself (as almost all comparisons to me do).

TRAIN YOURSELF TO TRAIN BETTER

12

I was training and improving, but I still didn't enjoy running, and I don't think it enjoyed me. However, I did discover another facet of running that I did enjoy—deciding where to run.

Running four times a week, it's easy to get bored of the same route. Furthermore, with my distances increasing, the same old routes weren't enough anymore. I needed miles, and the truth was, it wasn't that easy to find them. This must be how collectors of rare Cabbage Patch dolls feel as they desperately crave the 1984 Coleco baby boy Anthony Lindsey doll. They can't get it, just like I couldn't get miles. We are kindred spirits.

I NEED SOME MILES, MAN. I NEED 'EM BAD.

Before I started running, I didn't have a good sense of distance. How far was it from my house to a certain park? How far was my work? How far was the TV remote? I knew the relative distance, but I never realized the actual distance until I plodded along, watching the mileage on my running app slowly inch upward. Soon I understood where three miles was, but longer runs were still a mystery. If I set out

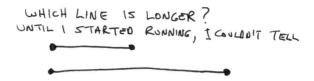

WHICH LINE IS LONGER?
UNTIL I STARTED RUNNING, I COULDN'T TELL

to run fourteen miles, I had to do some serious thinking beforehand to determine where I could run.

I thus found myself, pre-run and even mid-run, planning, doing math, wondering how many miles it would be if I took a different turn, added a detour, or just went somewhere new altogether. I was, in many ways, like a great explorer, running through uncharted territory, completely unafraid of whatever horrible threats I would come across, like a sprinkler, or even worse . . . a hill.

A quick note about hills: I love going downhill (shout-out to gravity for the constant assist), but I hate going uphill. The problem is, there's no way to avoid hills. They exist, and they are waiting to tax your legs and slow you down. Trust me, I personally have lost more time on hills than on Facebook.

Psyching myself up for hills before I left the house, I would put a few tiny mints in my pocket. I called these "hill pills" and told myself they had the power to push me up any incline. At the base of a hill, I'd pop one into my mouth, and fueled by chemicals that mimicked the flavor of peppermint, I would put my head down and get going. I know this is embarrassing. That's why I kept it to myself, and even now, it's between me and the two people who will read this book. If that's you, congratulations, you are in elite company.

TIP: As easy as it is to hate hills, it's good to run them. First, because they're like short interval runs, forcing you to change pace, intensity, etc., and second, because you can't avoid hills on any long run or race. Avoiding them now only makes meeting them later much worse, just like dentists and relatives.

Aside from hills, there was yet another wrinkle to my training I had to deal with. Normally in Los Angeles, wrinkles are immediately shot full of Botox, but I don't think that would work in this case because the wrinkle was training while traveling. I was occasionally out of town for work or personal reasons, yet I still needed to get my miles in. I tried running up and down the aisle of whatever airplane I was on, but

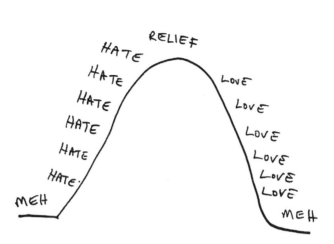

I found it dispiriting every time I was passed by a toddler doing the same thing.

Whatever hotel I was staying at, I would approach the front desk and ask the clerk for a running map. Most hotels have these for guests, and they show nearby popular and safe routes to run. Without fail, every time, the desk clerk would react with surprise that I, a soft, middle-aged bag of bloating, was even about to run at all. The only thing that may have been more surprising would be if I asked them to recommend a good local modeling agency.

In the interest of not rattling hotel employees, I found out that the running community anticipated the challenge of running in a strange city and solved it through the Internet. People all over the world have gone online to share favorite routes in every city on Earth. For example, if you ever find yourself in Madrid, merely enter "running route in Madrid" into a search engine. You're welcome to enter it even if you are not in Madrid; neither I nor the Internet is going to tell anyone.

Different routes, different sights, different elevations, different cities: All these helped raise my interest level a little while running, but still, I knew what I was doing—exercising. My brain was not about to sit around and let my body exercise. No way. Whenever it caught me running, my brain would unleash every nerve impulse it had to convince me I was bored. And it worked. Running was dull, a tedious chore, like paying bills but without the sex appeal. I knew I had to do something, and I did: I decided I was going to outwit my brain.

ASPIRE TO BE BRAIN-DEAD

13

Trying to think of a way to trick your brain isn't easy—everywhere I went, that jerk was there, listening in, seemingly aware of even my innermost thoughts. I tried everything: getting my brain drunk, showing it the complete *Twin Peaks* series to confuse it, even several concussions, but no matter what, my brain stayed with me every step of the way.

THIS is YOUR BRAIN ON BOOZE

I had heard stories of people who love running for the solitude and the mental clarity. You hear people talk about how running is where they find answers to the problems that vex them. This sounded good to me; I'm as vexed as anyone. I thus decided that's what I would do—use my running time to think.

On my next run, a long fifteen-miler, I made a determined effort to think, and indeed, I had a breakthrough—I realized my thoughts are stupid. Instead of sorting out the problems in my life, I wondered why football and hockey teams put their logos on baseball caps. Isn't this supporting baseball, the competition? Wouldn't this be like showing ads for TV shows in theaters before movies, or like running shoe companies

A MYSTERY FOR THE AGES

making shoes that simulate barefoot running? Oh wait, both of those already happen.

I consequently spent the rest of my run trying to decide if I was an idiot or a business genius. Even though I was biased to declare myself a genius, I couldn't. I knew I was just throwing good synapses after bad. Every thought I had was complete drivel. I was everything that was wrong with everything. Never again would I subject myself to my own ignorance. I needed a plan C. And here, finally, my brain came through.

The plan I came up with was a good one—distraction. I would fool my brain by feeding it. Not music, that's too easy to ignore. It had to be content that required attention so my brain wouldn't realize I was running. I downloaded every podcast I could and listened as I ran, and guess what? My brain fell for it. I distracted myself enough to run. Now I just have to hope that my brain doesn't hear about this book and learn what I've done. My brain has a baaaaad temper.

Loading up on podcasts that I hoped would be engaging, I started with several from NPR. If I wasn't going to get fitter or faster, I was definitely going to get more liberal. Luckily, before I hit leftist rock bottom, I discovered audiobooks. You may know them as books on tape, but that term is as antiquated as calling fire "heat on sticks."

There were countless audiobooks that were downloadable right to my phone, and they got me through a lot of runs. Some of the books were so good I wanted to listen to them while doing things I didn't hate, like not running, but I made a deal with myself that I could only listen to them while running. In case you are curious, a list of some of the better books and podcasts I listened to follows in a later appendix. This is supposed to encourage you to stick with this book all the way to the end—a carrot dangling at the end of the stick. I know it will work because there's nothing in the world more enticing than carrots, especially ones that have been tied to sticks.

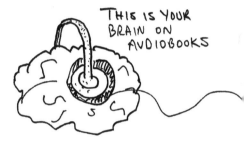

ALL ABOUT THAT PACE

14

> "I'm all about that bass . . ."
> —MEGHAN TRAINOR SONG
>
> (Even before I finished typing that chapter title, the song it's a pun of was already fading from popular memory. Instead of changing it to something with a little more staying power, I just typed faster.)

As you may remember, I ran the Santa Monica 5K race at a pace of about nine minutes per mile. A marathon is over eight times longer than a 5K, making me wonder what pace I should plan to run if I hoped to finish. There were a lot of things to consider.

From some of my longer training runs, I knew I felt more comfortable running at a pace of ten minutes per mile, but could I keep that up for 26.2 miles? If I couldn't, how fast would I walk once I inevitably had to stop running? How fast would I crawl? What would my pace be after my heart exploded? How fast would the ambulance be going as it rushed me to the hospital?

NOT "SPEED LINES" BUT "STINK LINES" THAT FELL OVER FROM BOREDOM

Instead of looking for a pace per mile, I started to think about what my total finishing time would be/should be/could be, so I could then divide and find my pace per mile. I looked online, searching "what is a good marathon time?" and again, the community of runners answered.

First, let's start with the fastest. For elite athletes, a good marathon time is just over two hours. The world record, in case you were wondering, was set in 2014 at 2:02:57. In the last hundred years, the fastest marathon time has dropped by about an hour, and then by about three minutes since 1998, but now any improvements are minimal, shaving just seconds off the previous record. One of the great books I read/listened to during training was *The Perfect Mile* by Neal Bascomb. The book details the quest to run a sub-four-minute mile and how close runners got before Roger Bannister finally broke the barrier in 1954. Nowadays, even some high school athletes have run sub-four-minute miles, and the world record is at three minutes, forty-three seconds. It's amazing to see that training, nutrition, evolution, and technology can make a huge difference in human performance, but at some point, the body reaches its performance limits. With the marathon, we seem to be at that limit.

The human animal currently can't make the subtle improvements needed to finish in less than two hours, even with the record just three minutes over. To get there, a runner would need a pace of about four minutes, thirty-four seconds per mile, which sounds crazy fast, but is actually just seven seconds per mile faster than the current record. Seven seconds off roughly four and a half minutes. It feels like that miniscule difference could come from shaving your legs or wearing a more form-fitting shirt, but even with my ridiculous ideas thrown in the mix, that slightly faster pace has been unattainable.

Just like the four-minute mile, the sub-two-hour marathon will eventually happen, probably even in my lifetime. (If you've heard the noises I make when I get up off a couch, you know this means it will happen soon.) I believe that right now, there is a little kid out there somewhere in the world who will grow up to do it. This kid just needs the right training, the right nutrition, and the right opportunities. Helping this kid would be so much easier if said kid would just step forward and identify themself, but apparently, our next great marathon runner is also a little shy.

I was still looking for the best pace for me, however, and looking at the fastest runners was a bit like looking at Formula One cars to help me make a decision about which bus pass to buy. For mortals, the snobby running purists online suggested that a "good" finishing time was anything less than four hours. Less than four hours? I agree that is a good amount of time for a flight or a workday, but less than four hours to run 26.2 miles seemed pretty quick.

Next I tried looking at the average time it took to run a marathon. According to a study done by British newspaper *The Guardian*, the global average finishing time in 2014 was 4:21:21. This was incidentally about forty seconds faster than the average time for the period from 2009 to 2013, which may support your cranky uncle's oft-repeated theory that "the whole damn world is going downhill." The country with the fastest average time was Spain (3:55:35), although this is a bit skewed because almost 94 percent of marathoners in Spain were male, and in general, men run faster than women. I'm sure your cranky uncle has a theory on why that is, but I won't repeat it here.

As a trivia note, the country with the slowest average marathon time is the Philippines (5:05:13). Reading this study is how I found out I'm from the Philippines. My parents, doctors, and passports had all been lying to me. I was furious.

Still, I was no closer to an answer. I wasn't going to set the world record, I wasn't a "true" runner, and I didn't even consider myself to be an average runner. Thus, I did what I do with any important life decision: I decided to mirror the behavior of a celebrity. Famous people are always the wisest! This logic explains why I wear an assortment of Mr. T necklaces, and also why I painted my wife blue in her sleep so I could feel like I was in *Avatar*.

Researching how fast various celebrities had run marathons, this is what I found:

Will Ferrell ran the 2003 Boston Marathon in 3:56. This is a pace of around nine minutes per mile, which I had already determined was too fast for me. I'd always suspected that Will Ferrell is better than me in every way. This confirmed it.

Katie Holmes ran the 2007 New York City Marathon in 5:29, averaging over twelve minutes per mile. Too slow for me, although I can imagine it gave her some nice "alone time" away from her now ex-husband, Tom Cruise.

Al Roker, the *TODAY* show weatherman, ran the 2010 New York City Marathon in 7:09. At around sixteen minutes per mile, the verb "ran" may be questionable here. Too slow for me.

The first celebrity time was too fast. The other times were too slow. It was all starting to feel like a running-based version of Goldilocks and the Three Bears. Further linking the two, both the story of Goldilocks and my marathon adventure have oatmeal in them. (Fans of oatmeal, hang on—there is another oatmeal mention coming up in a later chapter!)

Not finding a celebrity to pace myself against was frustrating, but as luck would have it, the fog of confusion soon cleared to reveal one iconic and inspiring role model—a person inspiring and iconic enough to exist at the "one name" level of fame. No, not Bono, Cher, Madonna, or Wisconsin. (Although, those four have all inspired me in different ways.) I'm talking about none other than *Oprah*.

Yes, Oprah. If you are a foreigner, or a caveman, or a foreign caveman, you may not know who Oprah is without her last name. If that's true, the Oprah I speak of is Oprah Winfrey, former TV talk show host, current billionaire. Among all of Oprah's amazing accomplishments, she also ran the 1994 Marine Corps Marathon in 4:29. This breaks out to be a pace of just about ten minutes per mile.

This running pace wasn't the only thing Oprah and I had in common. We'd both been to Chicago and Los Angeles—how many people can say that? It seemed to be destiny. She was the celebrity I would try to emulate. I wasn't the first to peg Oprah as my marathon muse. In fact, her marathon time had inspired many others. The time of four and a half hours is actually called the "Oprah line" by runners and is described on Wikipedia as "a notorious goal among the slower participants in marathons." Slower participants? That's me!

Then I did something radical. I decided I wasn't about to run at the same pace as Oprah; I was going to beat her—by a very slight margin! With that, I set my goal. I would finish in under 4:29, consequently running at just about ten minutes per mile.

Hear that, Oprah? Someone you don't know, and who never really watched your TV show, is challenging your time twenty years after you set it! Scared? I bet if I could get past your security and entourage to tell you this was happening, you would be!

Full of competitive spirit from this imaginary feud, I also learned that aside from the thrill of beating Oprah's time, finishing under 4:30 has the additional benefit of the *New York Times* including your name in their marathon results section the day after the race. Has Oprah ever had her name in the *New York Times*? I doubt it, but I was gonna!

SMART
TO FINISH

15

> "My feet have several thousand meetings scheduled with the dirt on a trail not far from here. Who am I to keep them waiting? Time to run."
> —UNKNOWN
>
> Unknown, I don't know a lot about management, but have your feet ever thought about hiring an assistant to wade through this overwhelming number of meetings to free up a little breathing room? Maybe your feet could start delegating a little bit, so other body parts can handle some of these meetings? I've tried to call your feet directly to suggest these ideas, but, as you might expect from someone with this workload, their voice mailbox is full.

I kept training, following the program prescribed on the app. As I pushed myself along, I realized six things, six nuggets of wisdom that I think merit being passed along. Why only six? Because six is the lazy man's equivalent of a top ten list. Anyway, here they are—six gems, all incredibly wise, true, and contradictory.

1) You can't run five miles unless you've already run four.
This is obvious, but sometimes obvious things need to be said. For example: "Your house is on fire!" In the context of running, my point is this—if you head out for the five-mile run you're supposed to do, don't quit at four miles. Don't quit when you are near your goal. If you've already made the effort to get 80 percent of the way there, that last 20 percent is a lot easier than doing the whole thing from scratch all over again. Push yourself to save yourself.

$$1 \quad 2 \quad 3 \quad 4 \quad 5$$

HEY, HE'S RIGHT!

2) Bad runs happen to good people.
You will go on a lot of runs. Some will be easy, and some will, for whatever reason, be really hard. You may leisurely run six miles one day, barely breaking a sweat, and then try to run three miles two days later and inexplicably feel like you are running with cement on your feet. Now, if in between these two runs you did something to annoy the mafia enough that they actually put cement on your feet, and they were

about to push you off a dock, but you escaped and are now running away with your feet encased in cement, the difference between these two runs makes sense. If this is indeed what happened to you, I suggest you stop reading and keep running—your life is in danger. However, for the rest of you, you are merely experiencing . . . the bad run.

I've had several bad runs. I've struggled, stumbled, and heaved just to finish an easy five miles. Those days, the way I ran, 26.2 miles seemed impossible. Sweaty and spent, it looked like my only chance to finish the marathon would be to convince the organizers to shorten the race to five miles. I knew this would be a monumental task, but maybe I could pull it off if I went to them with confidence and a really good PowerPoint presentation.

I had already done runs of ten and fifteen miles at that point, so why was this run so hard? It didn't make sense. Was it diet? Was it sleep? Was it eating something bad while I slept? To find out, I again looked online and learned that these swings in fitness are normal. Runners have good and bad runs, seemingly tied to no reason whatsoever. Even professional runners acknowledge that there are days they just don't have it. If these finely tuned machines can have bad runs, it shouldn't be a surprise that we poorly tuned non-machines do also.

The bottom line is: Don't get hung up on the bad runs. Performance on any individual run is not indicative of anything bigger than that specific run. Just believe in the program, believe in your training, believe in your improvement over time, and move on to the next run.

3) The first three miles are just warm-up.
No sane person would ever write that, or read that, but when you are training for a marathon, you have already abandoned your sanity. Still,

it's true. Of the many similarities between running and childbirth, I assume another one is this: It gets a lot easier after the first three. What I mean, specifically, is that I found every run I went on got a little easier after the first three miles. I think it just takes the body that long to settle in to the rhythm of what's happening, or it takes the body that long to surrender to what's happening. Either way, believing this "fact" kept me going for those first three miles. I suggest you also buy into this poorly researched fact—it may help you get past a tough beginning, too.

4) Celebrate what you did; don't dwell on what you didn't.

After your run, if you are down on your pace or distance or anything else, try to flash back to before you started running at all and think about how impressed your former self would be with running as far as you just did. Think about meeting that flabby, out-of-shape former self and what an inspiration you would be to them. Don't think about the time travel needed for this; it will only exhaust you, and clearly you are already exhausted. You couldn't even run your normal run.

5) You can't be done if you never start.

Since much of the best part of running for me is being done, it probably stands to reason that the worst part is getting started. Waking early, tired and lazy, getting up and out of the house to run takes a Herculean effort (and Hercules wasn't much of a jogger—he was all about weights, and if the whispers are true, steroids).

As hard as it is, force yourself out the door. Even if you end up running a shorter distance or a slower pace than you had planned, you still did more than not doing anything. Even if you don't beat your time or distance goal, you beat your laziness, and that's definitely something.

6. Just because you're alone, doesn't mean you're alone.
In the middle of your training, when you have weeks to go, things can look bleak. You may ask yourself, "Why am I doing this?"—a thought common to people both in the middle of hard runs and in the middle of getting neck tattoos. If you can't remind yourself why, find external reminders. Look at the Instagram feed of the marathon you are training for, or look online for personal stories of marathon finishers. If you still need more, go to YouTube. There, among the videos of people playing video games, falling off trampolines, or being Justin Bieber, are videos of people starting, running, and most important, finishing marathons. Seeing others do it made me want to do it also (interestingly, watching someone fall off a trampoline had the exact opposite effect).

EAT DISGUSTING THINGS

16

> "You are what you eat."
> —MOM-FRIENDLY ADAGE
>
> (Untrue, except for cannibals who eat other cannibals.)

Only a few weeks into my training journey, I was told that to complete my long runs, and certainly the marathon, I would need to ingest carbohydrates along the way. I imagined this meant I could nibble on a baguette as I ran, but then I thought about how a baguette isn't really that good without jam or butter. Plus I would need some silverware: That jam isn't gonna spread itself. And then I thought about the money I could make if I developed a self-spreading jam. So I booked a bunch of meetings with venture capitalists to pitch them my concept of self-spreading jam, but negotiations broke down over equity points and the fact that the whole idea was ludicrous. That was an exciting time in my life—I was laughed out of some really impressive offices. Luckily, smarter people than me have figured out an easier way for runners to fill up on carbs as they run. Unluckily, that answer is energy gels.

ENERGY GELS

Single-serving packages of high-carbohydrate sludge that help fuel the body in long endurance events. If you can't remember all of this, just remember "sludge."

I went to my local sporting goods store to buy some of these energy gels. There, I discovered that they come in an assortment of flavors, all meant to sound delicious: mocha, citrus, raspberry, etc. The array of flavors reminded me of being a kid in the dentist's chair when the hygienist would let me choose the flavor before putting the fluoride goo on my teeth. They had "bubble gum," "cotton candy," and "vanilla." (Curious how all these flavors were things a dentist really shouldn't be encouraging kids to eat.) Regardless, no matter which flavor I chose, as soon as the goo-filled trays went in my mouth, I would realize they don't taste at all like the flavor I was promised. I would sit there, drooling and gagging, my mouth full of a foul chemical mess, trying not to throw up. Well, let me tell you this: Most energy gels are worse than that.

I understand why the energy gel marketing guys spend so much time naming the flavors. They need great names to distract you from the texture: gluey, slimy, and exactly the wrong thickness. The texture of an energy gel is what scientists would come up with in response to people complaining that the texture of pudding is too enjoyable to eat.

To be fair, energy gels are carb-rich and dense. (The same could be said about me.) They are also necessary. (Can't be said about me.) The human body, I have been told, can't hold enough calories to get through a marathon without hitting "the wall."

THE WALL

In running lexicon, this is the point where your body surrenders to exhaustion, manifesting itself in various ways, including confusion, lack of motor control, etc. Runners also call this "bonking," a name that must have made sense to the originator, who presumably was bonking at the time he came up with it.

As a person who generally likes to stay in control of my motor skills, I didn't want to "bonk," so as I ran, I found myself ripping open energy gels and forcing lumps of this horrid gunk into my mouth, then quickly chasing it with water to try to get the taste out. Per the instructions on the gels, I did this every forty-five minutes. Some people do it even more frequently. I read that Lance Armstrong swallowed more than thirteen energy gels when he ran the 2006 New York City Marathon in just under three hours. I believe this to be true, because I know Lance Armstrong wouldn't lie about the things he put into his body.

Lastly, any discussion about energy gels raises the question of how to carry them. On a long run, you need a lot of them, and the runner accessory market has tried to address this need.

There are things you can buy to hold your gels called fuel belts, which are as about as attractive as they sound. The alternative method I read the most about involves safety pinning gels to your shorts, then rolling the shorts over and keeping the gels against your skin. This has the advantage of letting you rip the gel open as you pull it from your shorts, but it has the disadvantage of heating the gel up to the unpleasant human body temperature of someone running for a long time. If, by chance, you are a lizard with a low body temperature, this method may be perfect for you. As a non-lizard, it didn't work for me. Instead, I found a pair of shorts with a zippered pocket and put the gels in there. Unsexy, unfashionable, but it worked.

A word of warning about energy gels: If you eat too many, you run the risk of a problem some people lovingly call "goo-gut." On one of my runs, I had a brief affair with goo-gut, and like most affairs do, this one ended with me sitting on a toilet praying for a quick death. For the purposes of this book, however, goo-gut does offer a lovely segue into other bad things you can do to your body as you begin running long distances. Let's go there now.

DON'T GET HURT

17

> "You always hurt the one you love."
> —A MILLS BROTHERS SONG
> (See "chub rub.")

Injuries are going to happen. If you're not injured while running, you could slip in the shower and wrench your knee. I suppose you could also slip in the same shower again and fix the same knee (I don't understand how medicine or knees work—even showers are a bit of a mystery to me), but running more often puts you more often at risk of getting hurt. As I ran more, I got injured in every possible way, and with bad luck, you can, too! Thanks to clumsiness, or possibly extensive research for this book, I experienced the following:

General chafing: I think the first time most of us heard of General Chafing was in a history book. To remind you, he fought bravely in the Franco-American War, only to eventually die of a severe case of chub rub (read on). There is no better way to honor him than to go for a long run on Memorial Day in ill-fitting shorts.

Chub rub: Bonking, goo-gut—runners seem to have found cutesy names for horrible things. Were they around at the time, I am sure they would have described the Black Plague as "Bye-bye Die," or a gun-toting gorilla sniper as an "orangu-bang." Regardless, let me enter one more cutesy term into your lexicon: "chub rub."

Chub rub is the very real sensation of repeated friction chafing your undercarriage. How far under the carriage are we talking about? Think of the very nadir, between your legs. At least that's where I met chub rub. This area, in my experience, goes through a lot on longer runs, and none of it is good. In fact, if you ever see me walking gently and bow-legged with a prayer candle and flowers next to a picture of my once-healthy undercarriage, you will know what has happened— chub rub. It happened to me *every time* I ran more than six miles. Every. Single. Time.

After this happened to me dozens of times, I knew I had to do something. Then, after still not doing anything about it for another dozen times, I sprang into action. My first idea was organize a 5K run to support chub rub research, but that seemed a bit like having a toddler pie-eating contest to combat child obesity, so I decided to find the cure for chub rub myself. It didn't involve any medical work, but rather, typing "stop chafing during running" into a search engine. All my hard work was quickly rewarded—the solution to chafing was of all things named "anti-chafing balm." The prefix "anti" is a great way to know you've found the solution to a problem. Like antifreeze solves the problem of things freezing, and anticipation solves the problem of . . . cipation. Anyway, in this case, anti-chafing balm was just what the Internet ordered. And also exactly what I ordered over the Internet.

This was my first experience with anti-chafing balm, also known by its much more visual name, "body glide," but instinctively, I knew what I had to do. I suppose it was some reflex evolved through previous generations of chafed ancestors, but once I got that body glide in my hand, without hesitation, I began to smear it on my most delicate areas.

As I put it on for the first time, early in the morning, my running shorts down at my knees, giving myself a lube job, I had to ask myself, "What decision in my life has led me to this?" Epiphanies aside, I had been converted. Fourteen miles later I was miraculously chafe-free. Hallelujah.

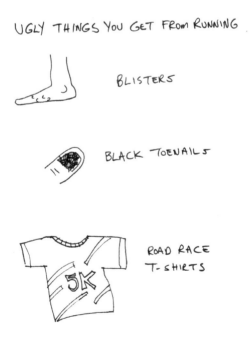

UGLY THINGS YOU GET FROM RUNNING

BLISTERS

BLACK TOENAILS

ROAD RACE
T-SHIRTS

HOW TO LOSE A MARATHON

The nail in the coffin: This is not a warning or even a prediction. This is fact. After repeated banging against the front of your shoes, some of your toenails will go black.

If you are goth and wear a lot of dark nail polish, you may not even notice this until the dead nail falls off. If you are an international spy who had the misfortune of being caught and tortured by bad guys who pulled off your toenails in an effort to make you talk, you also may not notice this. Perhaps now is a good time to say, I don't expect this book to be read by goth international spies. They are, of course, welcome to read it, but it isn't written specifically for them. I know they are a significant part of the book-buying market, but I've decided not to pander to them and, instead, stay true to who I am.

Plantar fasciitis: Everyone hates fascists (I presume), but plantar fasciitis may be even worse, simply because it is hard to cure and could mess up your marathon.

Plantar fasciitis is pain in a tissue that runs across the bottom of your foot. It's sometimes called "jogger's heel," but I once saw it called "policeman's heel," which thrilled me to think at least one part of my body could be a cop.

I got plantar fasciitis and can confirm it is painful, particularly for the first steps you take in the morning. I read about and tried many solutions including rolling my feet over a golf ball, and while I am sure that would defeat fascism, it didn't do a lot for fasciitis.

I tried some of the shoe inserts sold in that one aisle of the drugstore you never go down, and they didn't really work either. Neither did massaging balms and oils into the soles of my feet. The one thing that did work a little was elevating my feet for long stretches (i.e., being incredibly lazy). The pain never fully went away, but it lessened enough that I could run, which would bring some discomfort back, which led to me having to elevate my feet again. It was a wonderful, non-vicious cycle.

Sore nipples: This isn't just an awesome name for a band or a baby; it's also a real thing that plagues runners.

When I first started running, I never experienced any nipple pain, but then, like an idiot, I lost some weight. Once my XL shirts got a little looser, they would move more when I ran, and they started to rub against and irritate my most useless of all body parts—my nipples. For the record, I *want* to use my nipples more (I hate inefficiency), but my nipples never cooperate. Trust me, this subject will come up at my nipples' performance review later this year.

Perhaps not surprisingly, the answer to this upper-body chafing is the same as lower-body chafing: body glide, a.k.a. Vaseline, a.k.a. petroleum jelly. (Boy, nothing makes you want to apply something to your body like the word "petroleum," does it?)

Ankles, feet, hips, etc.: I always ran in the morning, and with the sun usually not up, I often found myself running in the dark. (Trivia note: "Running in the Dark" was never considered as an alternate title to the Springsteen song "Dancing in the Dark.") Running in the dark has its benefits; it's cool outside, and you can generally run on the road without many cars. The problem with running in the dark is that it is ... well, dark. You can't see as well as you might like. I once tried running with a headlamp, but I felt a bit like a coal miner, or a surgeon, or a surgeon who for some unsanitary reason insists on only doing operations in coal mines. More often than not, I ran without a headlamp and trusted the dim half-light I would get by holding my phone in front of me as I ran.

This idiotic solution was mostly fine, except for the times it wasn't. About three months into my training program, I was running in the dark, hit a pothole in the road, and dropped like a bag of sand. My phone broke my fall, and my fall broke my phone. That was an expensive accident, but miraculously, I had only a few scratches.

As I lay on the ground, scraped in a few places, I reassured myself that it could have been worse—someone could have seen my embarrassing fall. Right after I let that sink in, I heard, from across the street, "Are you OK?" Someone *had* seen my embarrassing fall.

Having my clumsiness witnessed was bad enough, but now this Good Samaritan was checking in on me. Loudly checking in on me. Checking in on me with much more than an "outside voice." This woman, a very kind hearted soul, had that rare type of voice that carries over distances.

I offered a little wave, trying to both signal that I was fine and that the matter was over. We'd all done our parts. She asked if I was OK, I waved, and now she should continue walking her dog, and I should limp home. That wasn't to be. No, this Good Samaritan was a little *too* good. In her lovely, caring foghorn of a voice, she asked again, even louder this time, "Are you OK?" I ran through my options and realized that aside from being rude or pretending I don't speak English—or pretending I was both rude and a non-English speaker (i.e., French)—I had to answer. I told her, "I'm fine, thanks." She seemed content to leave it there, but then I made the mistake of standing up.

As soon as I stood, this new high-volume friend saw my legs, knee, and wrist were covered in blood. I wasn't hemorrhaging; I had only a few small scrapes, but when put together, the cumulative effect was of three tiny murder scenes. I could hear her gasp all the way on my side of the street. Her dog may have gasped, too. She looked me over again and then said the only thing she could have—"ARE YOU OK?"

She didn't just "say" it; she broadcast it. Avalanches and air raid sirens are quieter than the voice she used. The next thing we both knew, lights came on in nearby houses, doors opened, and people came out to see if I was OK. My little stumble soon led to me telling an audience of people in their bathrobes that indeed, I was OK.

My point is, little or big things can and do happen. In this instance, my hearing was hurt more than my body, and it was a good thing, because I had more training to do. The marathon was just a month away, and getting hurt would have been a disaster. It would have meant I did all this training for nothing other than fitness and self-esteem.

Reading the book to this point (one of us has to do it), I realize I've highlighted only bad things about running, like boredom and injuries. Now it's time to talk about the good stuff.

APPRECIATE THE GOOD STUFF

18

> "No one ever drowned in sweat."
> —LOU HOLTZ, LEGENDARY COLLEGE FOOTBALL COACH
> (Also, what a lifeguard told me after I waved for help while running at the beach.)

While I never felt the adrenaline-fueled euphoria others do, there were, and are, many positive things that came from running. The first, of course, was fitness. Both my house and workplace have a lot of stairs, and before I started running, I would take them in stages, stopping halfway like I was at a Mount Everest base camp. There, I would pause and catch my breath before I made a charge for the summit. This ceased to be a problem after I started running.

I was also losing weight. My whole life I had lost at sports, and now I was losing something I could be happy about. While I plodded along slowly, the weight dropped off fast. From the time I started training to the start of the marathon, I lost over twenty pounds. That may sound like a lot, but don't worry, after I stopped running as much, I found several of those pounds again. (They were hiding at the bottom of an ice cream container.) Sure, I'm still down ten or so pounds, but that's what insurance is for, right?

Running didn't only make me thinner; it also made me more toned. Even though most of the actual effort in running is in the legs, I found my arms, core, back, and other muscles benefitted as well. One day, I even saw that my feet had some noticeable muscle definition. That's right, I had muscles in my feet. My previously obese paws now looked like the buff, ripped feet of a dainty She-Hulk.

I also think running improved my posture, because suddenly people were telling me I looked taller. If this continued, interested NBA scouts would be coming around, only to leave again when they saw I can't even hit the rim on a free throw.

Better health, posture, and stair climbing were the little signs of encouragement I needed, because the race was looming, less than a month away. My training continued, my mileage and pace increased, and then mercifully, I came to the absolute best part of the marathon training experience—the taper.

What? Something in this training can get *less*?! I was overjoyed, but I was also worried. Would I fall out of whatever shape I worked so hard to get myself in? How much taper is too much? How much is too little? Even if I do taper correctly, how much of a benefit will it give me?

As thorough as my training program was, it wasn't full of information about the taper. Rather, in my app's little daily encouragement/ advice section, when it came to the taper, it simply read, "Take it easy, the hay is in the barn." As a nonfarmer, this only confused me more. Is the hay supposed to be in the barn? Don't the animals eat the hay? Are the animals also in the barn? Any chance I can sell this barn? How about an insurance fire? I bet all that hay would burn things up pretty good and then—*ka-ching*!

I tried to read as much as I could about tapering and discovered a lot of people talking about "taper madness."

TAPER

The gradual lessening of training so the legs are fresh and ready for race day.

TAPER MADNESS

A restless feeling due to an excess of energy since none is being expended running.

CARBO-LOADING

Basically and unscientifically, the idea of eating as many carbs as possible, to stuff glycogen into every open spot in your metabolism. During the race, this glycogen will be converted to glucose, giving you energy.

As detailed previously, an excess of energy has never been my problem, although I am keeping "taper madness" as a handy excuse for any future crime I commit. (My attorney: "Your honor, my client didn't know what he was doing—he was all hopped up on taper!")

Regardless, I had no choice but to trust the program. This was easy to do when I reminded myself that the program was written by Jeff Gaudette, a man who has coached thousands of runners and has run Olympic Trials qualifying times himself. I, on the other hand, once threw out my back reaching for a sweater.

So I chose to see the taper for what it was—a mental and physical oasis. I hadn't had the struggle of the race yet, but I did have the success of completing the training program. When I told this to an experienced runner, they corrected me on something. They pointed out that the taper is still part of the training program. The rest was getting me ready for the race as much as the runs had. To a sloth-ophile like me, this was amazing. As I lay on the couch, I wasn't just watching reality TV shows about the untold fortunes waiting in abandoned storage lockers; I was, in fact, still training. And let me tell you, this part of the training I excelled at; I nailed every channel change, DVR series set, and commercial fast-forward like a true champ.

I learned that there was yet one more amazing part of all this training. With only a week before the race, I found out it was time to carbo-load.

There are different opinions on how long one should carboload and what percentage of your meal should be made up of carbs. I chose to make my average meal about 90 percent carbs, ignoring any research that disagreed with my vision of me charging through the city, gobbling up everything that had flour in it—a Carb-zilla, if you will.

I jammed my craw full of every piece of bread, pasta, or other carb I could find. I knew I had really found the carbo-load zone the night I sat down to my own recipe of beer-battered penne in a bread bowl, with breadsticks as utensils and a large glass of cookie dough as a drink. A wonderful night, until I blacked out.

Sitting on my ass, eating carbs, I had trained for fifteen weeks to get the exact lifestyle I had before I even started running.

Hakuna matata.

DON'T GET HURT 2: THE INJURING

19

> "Tough times don't last. Tough people do."
> —A.C. GREEN, PLAYED IN 1,192 CONSECUTIVE NBA GAMES
>
> (Don't forget beef jerky, that lasts a long time, too.)

As I headed out on an early morning for one of the last few runs before I would leave for New York, I was feeling good. I felt strong, and dare I say, I felt a little confident. Then I felt something else—severe pain.

The pain was coming from my ankle. I had turned it. I suppose the term "turning your ankle" exists because the physical act is literally turning the ankle over awkwardly, but I would also believe the term exists because I had turned my ankle from a perfectly functioning ball of bone and ligaments into a useless, painful ball of nothing.

It was still dark when it happened, and that was a good thing, because when I stepped on that uneven sidewalk crack, I dropped like a lead piano. I landed on a threadbare patch of grass and proceeded to scream like a teenage girl who had just met One Direction, and then each member of the band kicked her in the ankle. It was bad. Really bad.

I lay there for about thirty minutes waiting for the pain to subside. And when it did, I stood up, and the pain came right back. With no other alternative, I began limping the two miles back to my car. Each step was pure agony.

I'd turned my ankle before, so I knew the only remedy was to wait. I also followed the R.I.C.E. method (an acronym for rest, ice, compression, elevation). At this point I was on board with any medical treatment named after carb-heavy food.

Days passed, my anxiety level and my ankle stayed elevated, and then they both started to lessen enough that I was determined to finish off my last few runs. Just to be safe, I went to my local drugstore and purchased a therapeutic ankle support. I know there is no sexier combination of words in the English language than "therapeutic," "ankle," and "support," but seeing this thing would have cooled off any feelings the name may have aroused. It was a small, beige, elastic ankle cuff— the bastard child of an Ace bandage and a spat, with none of the chic design. I pulled it on my inflamed ankle and it pretty much worked. With it, I was able to get in those last few runs, and then it was suddenly time to go to New York.

THE
QUEST
BEGINS

20

> "The difference between try and triumph is a little *umph*."
> —MARVIN PHILLIPS, MINISTER AND MOTIVATOR
>
> (A for inspiration, D for spelling.)

My family had been incredibly supportive during my training—I was often out running when they woke up, and my wife had to handle breakfast on her own before I came home, sweaty and exhausted. For them, the exciting part of my marathon was going to be the trip to New York that came with it. I even promised them that, if we could find one, we would try to see a Broadway production that wasn't based on a Disney movie.

And then, a few days before the race, one of my daughters got sick, as kids do. Not bad sick, but sick enough that a long flight wasn't going to be a good idea. So my wife was now staying home with her. I could try to take my other daughter with me, but what would I do with her during the marathon? Those BabyBjörn thingies that hold a child up against your chest aren't allowed in the race. Trust me, if they were, I would have experienced the marathon snug against some burly man's pecs, playing games on my phone while he did all the work.

Recognizing babysitting wasn't practical, the only decision was to leave the entire family at home. Suitcase in hand and ankle in pain, I went off to the airport by myself.

As a frequent United flyer, I'm used to flight delays, and at LAX, I was told I would have to endure yet another one. In my mind, United is less of an airline than a collection of gypsy cab–like planes. I believe anyone out there with an airplane can just paint the United logo on the side and pick up some passengers. (This is just a joke. United planes are not like gypsy cabs. In gypsy cabs, you have legroom.)

Ever the optimist, I chose to see this low-rent flight as the first test of my marathon experience. The flight from Los Angeles to New York is about five hours; about as long as I expected the marathon to be. If I could make it through those five trying hours of recirculated air, uncomfortable seats, and desperately avoiding conversation with the person next to me, the marathon would be a breeze.

I eventually made it to New York and to my hotel, which was just off Times Square. The room was loud and offered a terrific view of the back of a billboard. The back. I had paid Manhattan hotel prices and I couldn't even enjoy the luxury of advertising staring me in the face. The room was also small, as New York hotels are, but it had all I needed—a bed where I could rest my still-aching ankle. I collapsed onto it, elevating my leg, and there I lay, wondering if it would be ready to run on. I would occasionally take a break to wonder what was on the other side of the billboard and then go back to wondering about the ankle again. It had to be ready for the marathon, but it also had to be ready for the next day, because that was when I would meet my Shoe4Africa teammates at an introductory brunch. Knowing the value of first impressions, I really wanted my ankle to look its best.

HOW TO LOSE A MARATHON

TEAMWORK MAKES THE DREAM WORK

21

> "There's no 'I' in 'team,' but there is in 'win.'"
> —MICHAEL JORDAN, NBA LEGEND
>
> (Instead of inspirational, this quote's actually kind of selfish, another word with an "I" in it—just like "forfeit," "quit," and, if you spell it wrong, "loser.")

Remember when the only way I got into this race was by joining a charity team? I don't. But I went back and reread this book, gave it a scathing review online, and then remembered that not only had I joined a team, but that we actually had a couple of team events. The first was our brunch and shakeout run.

We gathered at a nice restaurant off Central Park. There were about fifty people and, more interesting to me, a ton of carbs. Before my over-eating could begin, we were each given our team shirts. We put them on and then as a team, we ran a "light" couple miles through the park. Trying to keep everyone together, we ran at what was described as a "slow, ten-minute-mile" pace. That's right, their slow pace was my fast pace. This was not the encouragement I needed the day before the race.

As we ran through the park, we passed several other teams, also all wearing their matching team shirts, also doing their slow runs at my race pace.

When we got back to the restaurant I decided if I trailed the pack in the run, I would lead the pack in carbo-loading. I'd only been training for the marathon for four months, but I'd been training to gorge myself my whole life. I was a thing of beauty, smoothly moving from the pastries to the bagels to the muffins. At one point I even had three muffins in one hand—highlight reel material. After eating my second bagel, I thought about doing some sort of touchdown dance, but I stopped myself since that probably wasn't very good team behavior.

Finally, after my jaw muscles cramped and I stopped eating, I got to meet some of my teammates. I met a lovely Irish woman who was also running her first marathon; she had traveled to New York with her father, who was proud to be cheering for her. I met a New Yorker who asked me how many half marathons I had run to prepare for the race. I could have lied and said "a hundred and fifty thousand," but this was my teammate. I owed him the truth. I hadn't run any. I had run 13.1 miles

In the old days, that would be me running out to get a milkshake, but for runners it's a light jog the day before a race to stretch and warm up your muscles.

(half marathon distance) several times, but I never timed myself. He told me it didn't matter, but I could tell he was worried for me, because that's what teammates do.

The last teammate I met was from Germany. I don't honestly remember much about our conversation other than that he had recently been in Washington, DC, heard there was a marathon that day, and just walked over and signed up. No extra training, no planning—it just struck him as something to do that day. It's like he was looking at movie times and didn't see anything interesting, so he decided to run a marathon. He ran that marathon (and New York) in just over three hours.

Before we all split off, our team "coach" gave us a few last-minute tips about the course, told us things to watch out for, and reminded us to start slow so as to not burn ourselves out. I waited for him to whisper to me something like "slow for them, normal for you." But he didn't.

We would all see one another again that night at a team pasta party to grab some last-minute carbs, but before I could even think about that, I had other business to attend to. I assume my German teammate spent his afternoon before the marathon running another marathon, but not me. I had to go to the expo.

SURVIVE
THE EXPO

22

> "A twelve-minute mile is just as far as a six-minute mile."
> —UNKNOWN
>
> (I wish I knew who said this. I'd propose marriage to them.)

I had no idea what a marathon "expo" was. Now that I do, I miss those earlier days of blissful ignorance.

The first thing I came to understand about the expo is that it's a scam. If that seems harsh, perhaps "racket" is a better word. I choose these hurtful descriptions only because they are accurate. You see, you have to go to the expo to pick up your race bib. Read that again—you HAVE to pick up your bib there—you have no other choice. If you want to run the race, you need to go to the expo.

Once you are at the expo, you will quickly see that you have been lured into a trap. You have been drawn deep into a makeshift bazaar where tracksuit-wearing vendors hawk souvenirs, shoes, and everything else. Just like every other experience in America, the marathon has a gift shop, and this is it.

TIP: Stay off your feet as much as you can the day before the race. At the expo, get your bib and get out.

I ignored the tip I just wrote. Ignored it big time. Curious and stupid, after I got my bib, I wandered.

There were free samples of food, some of it only marginally related to running. Grazing, in the span of two minutes I ate a "power candy" and some string cheese. I was instantly energized and constipated.

There was a booth selling sweat-proof earphones, another selling motivational headbands, and another selling sneaker charms. These weren't your regular sneaker charms—these featured the logo of your favorite NFL team. I quickly thought about the mental boost I would get from looking down and seeing the iconic and inspirational Jacksonville Jaguars logo bouncing back at me. I kept walking.

There were also booths trying to get people to sign up for other marathons in exotic locations: London! Stockholm! Grand Rapids,

Michigan! There were booths selling clothes, discount sneakers, miracle injury-recovery cures, and, of course, there was the booth that exists at every trade show I've ever been to—the booth that no one goes to.

I forget what exactly this incarnation of that booth was selling, but I do remember how desolate it was. As is also common to this booth, there was a well-meaning person sitting there, hoping, desperately trying to make eye contact with anyone who walks by. Their hope quickly turns to bitterness as the target doesn't even turn to look or break their stride. That's when the bitterness turns to anger, manifesting itself in a narrow-eyed glare. I walked by this booth, experienced this cycle of emotions, and continued on with the satisfaction of knowing both the booth attendant and I had fulfilled our destinies. The circle was complete.

TIP: One booth I actually do endorse is the one that offers race photos. The company present at my race (and I've heard at many major marathons) is conveniently named MarathonFoto. They may not be able to spell "photo" correctly, but in my experience, they do everything else well. They have photographers and cameras positioned throughout the course and sell you high-quality photos and video of you taken throughout the race, including as you (hopefully) cross the finish line. They are terrific souvenirs, and if you spontaneously combust at mile fifteen, they're great for your next of kin to submit to the insurance company. At the expo they offer a discount on the photo package, which you are probably going to end up purchasing afterward anyway at full price. If you decide not to get the photo package there, don't worry; you will get about ten emails after the race showing you the photos and trying to sell them to you then.

Just like there is always a custodian supply closet you can hide in at a shopping mall, there was also the occasional non-retail oasis at the expo where some actual helpful things were happening. The first of these I discovered was a booth organizing pace teams.

There were teams for all different paces, and I thought about joining one, but ultimately I decided to run on my own. I was already about to disappoint one team; I didn't want to drag down another. Instead, I just optimistically grabbed one of the paper wristbands they offered that laid out the pace of a 4:30 marathon, specifying at what time I should cross each mile marker. Even if I ended up disappointing the wristband, still, I wasn't about to pass up free jewelry!

PACE TEAMS

Formed for a single race, these offer the chance to run with an experienced runner who guarantees to lead the team across the finish line at a specific time. It's a great idea for people that aren't sure how to pace themselves, and kudos go out to whoever thought it up (great job, un-researched guy!).

The expo also featured a series of lecturers speaking to the nervous first-time marathoner like me. I took a seat in the audience, hoping to learn and rest my ankle. I can tell you now, I did both.

One speaker began by announcing to the crowd that we had "already lost the battle against dehydration, even before running a step." This was not the greatest pep talk I've ever heard (unless, of course, I was the sensation of dehydration—in that case, I would have walked out of there feeling pretty good!).

This same lecturer, who was preaching the importance of staying hydrated, went on to warn us about something called "hyponatremia," where you can drown yourself from drinking too *much*. Hearing this, I now had a new goal for my marathon. Ideally, I would finish, beat Oprah's 4:29 time, and, if everything went right, I wouldn't drown while exercising on dry land.

If you are about to run a marathon and are suddenly worried about dying from hyponatremia, let me tell you, it is very rare, but a concern you should look into all the same. If it makes you feel any better, I didn't look into it at all and (spoiler alert!) I didn't die.

THIS GUY NEEDS TO HYDRATE MORE

THIS GUY NEEDS TO HYDRATE LESS

From the perils of dehydration to the perils of over-hydration, this expert went on to tell us how we will know when we are hydrated just enough. It turns out the key to finding that sweet spot is looking at the color of your urine.

I found this a bit odd. There were more than a hundred adults, sitting calmly, talking about the color of their urine. A group critique of urine color isn't something that happens to me every day. It may be commonplace to you, in which case, my friend, you are into some funky stuff.

Going on, the expert described the perfectly hydrated color of urine as an off-white, almost an "eggshell." Never one to trust my own judgment, I thought about getting paint chips from a hardware store just so I could be sure the color was matching. What if I was emitting a "Winter Morning" white, or a "Scotch Mist," or even worse, a "Splendid Ivory"?! In the end, I decided to not worry too much about the color of my urine, and to literally and psychologically just "go with the flow."

MARATHON EVE

23

After the expo, I went to the team pasta party, filled up on carbs and small talk, and then headed back to my hotel. There, I ordered some pasta up to the room. After all, it had been almost an hour since I ate a full meal of carbs.

As I felt the bulge of carbs move through my body like a wild boar through a python, I had the last prerace phone conversation with the family (daughter getting better, thanks for asking). They wished me luck, we hung up, and then, like a teenage girl before the first day of school, or like a middle-aged man before his first marathon, I laid out my outfit for the next day.

I breezed through the shorts and socks portion of this task, but choosing a shirt wasn't as simple. I had three separate choices.

First choice was the shirt they give everyone when they pick up their bibs at the expo. As far as running shirts go, this one was unusual because it wasn't ugly. It was a pleasing shade of blue with a logo and the text "New York City Marathon" on the front. The problem came with the back of the shirt. There, printed in uppercase letters, was "FINISHER." I hadn't finished anything yet (aside from several plates of pasta). I didn't know how tomorrow was going to go. What if I didn't finish? The shirt was more optimistic than I was, and for that reason, it was out.

My second choice was the shirt my team gave me: a nice, white, wicking shirt with "Shoe4Africa" on the front. A lot of runners choose to write their names on the shirt they are running in. It gives the spectators a chance to cheer you on by name, and I am sure that it's helpful and motivating to hear, "Go Cindy," or, "You got this, Steve," particularly if your name is Cindy or Steve. I did not write my name on my shirt. I think I was afraid that if I did, someone may come across me somewhere in Brooklyn, slumped over and vomiting, and they would say something like, "That's it. Get it all out, Joel," or, "Let me hold your hair, Joel."

Still, the shirt was in contention. The good thing about it was that it had long sleeves, the weather was going to be cold, and it would help support the charity foolish enough to allow me on their team. The concern was that the shirt would irritate a twosome I was very close to and had grown up with. No, not my parents or my two brothers—I am talking about my nipples. I had never run in this shirt before, and I didn't know how much it might chafe.

TIP: Don't try or wear anything in the marathon you haven't tried or run with many times before. You don't want any surprises.

My third choice was the shirt I had run in many times before. It fit, it was also wicking, and it had an understanding with my nipples where they wouldn't bother the shirt, and the shirt wouldn't bother them.

I went back and forth between the team shirt and the reliable stand-by, and then, like a foolish King Solomon, I chose them both. I would wear the nipple-friendly standby and put the long sleeve Shoe4Africa shirt over top.

With my clothes chosen, I started laying out the other things I needed to take with me. Soon the bed was covered with more items than if I was trekking into the Amazon: my phone, aspirin, gels, head-phones, etc. I jammed all of this crap into the pockets of my shorts. They bulged to capacity, and I realized I was running the Burro Days World Championship Pack Burro Race after all, except I was the burro.

SHIRT   SHORTS

SOCKS   CRAP

Lastly, I took a pen, and with premeditated serial killer concentration, I wrote my fuel strategy on my pace bracelet. Yes, I had a fuel strategy, just like another one of my heroes, OPEC. Mine, however, was a plan to remind me when and where I should be taking an energy gel. All this busywork kept my thoughts off what was happening the next day—yet another way to fool my mind. What a sucker!

After another carb-rich snack, it was about 8 P.M. I set the alarm for 5 A.M. and went to bed. For a guy about to run a marathon, I had adopted the bedtime of a senior citizen. I pulled up the covers, closed my eyes, and then lay there wide-awake for the next couple of hours. I couldn't sleep. Doubts started creeping in: Can I do this? What about the taper? What about my ankle? What if my pace is off? Did I carbo-load enough? Did I carbo-load too much? What if I forget my body glide and the friction "down under" saws right through my body?

It wasn't long before my body contained an equal mix of worries and carbs. And then, as always happens when you lie awake full of worry, I also started to worry about not getting enough sleep. Worries had suddenly overtaken carbs in the ratio.

Time slipped away until finally I found solace in something I had heard at the expo that really resonated with me: a concession vendor yelling, "Pretzels!"

As I ate that pretzel, I heard something else that also gave me solace. It was a lecturer who told his audience that they might not think they are ready for the race, but they are. He encouraged everyone in the anxious group to look back at all their training, to go back and look at the stats of every run they'd done and see all the time they had put in to prepare. He went on to say the race itself wasn't a chore—the training was. The race was the reward you gave yourself for the all the chores you'd done. All those early-morning and late-night runs were just so you could do this race, and now, here it was.

So, I got out of bed and I did just that. I looked over all my runs. Damn, I did a lot of them. It made me feel better. I calmed down a little bit. I even started to believe that I was ready. And even if I wasn't, I recognized that I was at least at the point where I was tired of dwelling on this. Whatever was gonna happen, was gonna happen, so let's let it happen already!

1:00 A.M.

Nerves calmed, I fell into a peaceful slumber. That lasted about two hours, until . . .

3:12 A.M.

I bolted awake, worried that I didn't join a pace team. Maybe I should have joined the 4:30 team. Maybe the 4:15, or maybe even the 4:00. Maybe I've been underestimating myself! This is clearly that famous 3:12 A.M. bravado no one ever talks about. I was being ridiculous. I calmed my breathing using a few Lamaze exercises I remember from my daughter's birth, and then I fell back asleep. For about forty minutes.

4:00 A.M.

I was up again, my mind racing, thinking about how soon my body was about to be racing. I realized now there was no way I was going to get back to sleep, so I went to the bathroom to check my urine color.

When I saw the color, it was *not* what was described yesterday. I was riddled with shame! I had disappointed so many people. I started drinking water right then, hoping to salvage things.

4:30 A.M.

Good news! I was doing well. *Very* well. Sadly, this success was only in the baseball game I was playing on my iPad. I was playing against New York. New York—the city I was about to run "against." Freaky, right? Did you just get a chill? It could be the symbolism, or it could be your air conditioning, or maybe the onset of a horrible sickness. If you think it's the sickness thing, you should really see a doctor. It's very hard for me to diagnose you through a book.

5:00 A.M.

My alarm went off. Time to get up and lube up! I assume this is a line from the movie *Cars*—I never saw it. It may also be a line from some other movies, the type where they assure you the title won't show up on your hotel bill, but I've never seen them, either.

5:05 A.M.

I turned on my computer and saw that my inbox contained some encouraging emails from friends, plus another one telling me I was paying too much for car insurance. Full of self-doubt again, I chose to believe the only sincere message was about the car insurance.

5:10 A.M.

I checked my urine color again. It was perfect. I thought to myself, "I'm gonna win this thing!"

5:30 A.M.

Room service arrived with a banana and some oatmeal. Remember, oatmeal lovers, how I said oatmeal would make an appearance later in the book? Well, this is it! Congratulations! Worth the wait, right?

5:45 A.M.

Go time.

THE LONGEST JOURNEY BEGINS WITH A SINGLE CAB RIDE

24

> "It always seems impossible until it's done."
> —NELSON MANDELA
>
> (I'm not going to make fun of Nelson Mandela. No way. I'm not that much of a jerk. I will resume making fun of other accomplished people's quotes next chapter.)

I took a cab from the hotel to the terminal for the Staten Island Ferry. With a crowd of other marathoners, I climbed onto the ferry and traveled across New York Harbor toward Staten Island. From my seat I first had a great view of the Statue of Liberty, and then had a great view of all the other runners' butts as they stood in front of me to see the Statue of Liberty.

At Staten Island, we were hustled off the boat and lined up to board buses that would take us to Fort Wadsworth, the staging area where we would wait for the race to start. It was then that I realized the finish of the race, in Central Park, was about eight blocks from my hotel. Therefore I had taken a cab, a boat, and a bus to put me in a position to run right back to where I had started.

We got off the bus, and lined up for security checks. This was the first New York City Marathon after the Boston Marathon bombing just eight months before. While the fear of another horrible terrorist act may have scared some people off, I actually felt better thinking that security would be tighter than ever before—and it was. There were metal detectors, explosive-sniffing dogs, and tons of police officers. I felt completely safe from any bodily harm other than what I was about to do to my body myself. Why didn't the police stop me?

Fort Wadsworth started as a military blockhouse in 1663 and remained a military post until 1994, when it became the national recreation area it is today. This concludes the historical background on Fort Wadsworth. I'd like to tell you more, but at this point, I need to conserve my energy—I'm about to describe a marathon!

At Fort Wadsworth, we would all be separated into corrals. First to leave would be the wheelchair athletes, who are surprisingly fast—most finish in just over an hour and a half. Next out were the elite runners, who would finish in just over two hours. Not participating in either of these two waves is how I learned I was neither elite, nor in a wheelchair. Frankly, both were a shock to me.

As the other fifty thousand runners and I hung out, we were treated to free bagels, free tea, and also free long lines to use the free portable toilets. In fact, there were hundreds of toilets brought in just so we runners could line up at them, and we didn't disappoint. People lined up, used the bathroom, and then got back in line to do it all again. You can imagine that you want to empty your system as much as you can before the race, and repeated trips to the bathroom were efforts to do just that. I participated in this odd, repetitive pilgrimage, if only to ensure that I wouldn't have to stop the race for any reason other than my lungs turning to dust.

TIP: The multitude of people using the toilets prerace can lead to them being out of toilet paper. A wizened old runner thus told me to make sure I brought my own toilet paper, so I did. I wasn't alone in this. At a drug store in Manhattan the day before the race I saw many people buying body glide, aspirin, and toilet paper. They were either in the marathon or into some weird stuff I couldn't even imagine, and I have a pretty good imagination.

After a few repeat visits to the bathroom, I looked at my watch and saw it was time to wait some more. So I did. I took this opportunity to mingle a little bit with some people who would be running with me, or more likely, running in front of me.

I met one woman who told me she had run 110 marathons and even some triathlons. This was surprising, because she really didn't look like an amazing athlete. But apparently she was one, or she was an amazing liar. Either way, I was impressed.

I met a couple who were running their four hundredth marathon. Yes, four hundred marathons—you read that right (or at least I know I wrote it right—what happens from the page to your eyes is out of my control).

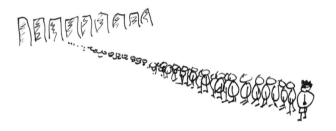

DISTANCE TO FINISH: 26.2 miles
DISTANCE TO TOILET: 2.62 miles

TIP: To stay warm prerace, buy some cheap sweats and a sweatshirt, and then donate them right before the race to the charities positioned at the staging area to collect exactly this type of clothing. At Fort Wadsworth several lovely charity workers gamely chanted, "Take it off," to the thousands of people removing jackets and sweatpants moments before the race. I obliged, performing a very slow burlesque dance that culminated in me having to sit down to take my sweatpants off over my running shoes. Truly a feast for the eyes.

An announcement then told me mingling time was over; it was time to get into the corral. It wasn't going to be long now.

MARATHON

25

> "It's not a sprint, it's a marathon."
> —PROVERB
>
> (I know this is a proverb, but here it's also a fact. Just like if you were out moss collecting and thought rolling a stone along the forest floor was a good method until a moss-collecting expert told you, "A rolling stone gathers no moss." It doesn't make it any less true, just a lot less poetic.)

Waiting for the race to start, I was overcome with nerves one more time. This was 26.2 miles. Way more than I had ever run before. I don't even usually drive that far. What had I gotten myself into? Could I actually do this?

I once again thought about the training I had put in, and how heartbreaking it would be give up now. Spurred on by determination, competitiveness, and mostly the thought of how much it would cost to take a cab all the way back to Manhattan, I was ready to go.

Each wave of the marathon is officially launched with speakers blasting out "New York, New York," and by firing off a cannon. When I heard them, I realized that either my race was starting, or I was in the middle of a Frank Sinatra concert that had been attacked by pirates. As ridiculous as the latter sounds, ten months before, me running a marathon sounded even more ridiculous.

The cannon went off, and I stumbled forward. Holy crap, I was running a marathon.

MILE 1

As mentioned previously, the marathon goes through all five boroughs of New York City, but the Staten Island part is a bit of a cheat. Sure, you spend the most time there, in Fort Wadsworth, waiting and repeatedly going to the bathroom, but when the race starts, the first mile immediately takes you out of Staten Island over the Verrazano-Narrows Bridge. As I ran over the bridge, I felt bad for the short shrift Staten Island was getting, but I also felt pretty pumped. I had already completed one of the five boroughs and still had jump in my legs.

Since this is the first bridge on the course, it's a great chance to insult bridges (I hope no bridges are reading this). Bridges are great for traveling over water and everything, but the big ones are also secretly hills, demanding the same effort any hill does. I realized this right away, with the Verrazano-Narrows Bridge. It's not only the longest bridge on the course, but also the longest suspension bridge in the United States. These two pieces of trivia are great to start a conversation with someone running next to you. (Probably less great if you are trying to start a conversation with a Russian supermodel in an Ibiza nightclub.) Either way, the race had just begun, and I was already climbing a hill hiding in a bridge's body.

Once off the bridge, I was in Brooklyn, the second borough. From there, we would run through Queens, the Bronx, and then, of course, into Manhattan. I had been to New York a few times, but I had never been outside of Manhattan, so I was interested to see these other boroughs. This tourism was proving to be yet another way to distract my mind from what my legs were doing, and I saw that I wasn't alone. Many people in the race were foreigners who were stopping frequently to take photos. This was their way of seeing a foreign city, checking out the sights while also sweating and nearly dying. I began to conceive of a line of postcards that could be sold during the race. Instead of saying, "Wish you were here," they could read, "Wish you were here with a sofa," or, "Wish you had stopped me from being here," or, of course, "Can you believe some idiot tried to sell me a postcard during a marathon?"

MILE 2

Now firmly in Brooklyn, I started to settle down. The race wasn't such a novelty anymore. I'd seen the crowds, run a bridge, and was still mostly alive. I didn't know how or when this was going to end, but I decided I had better take a moment to soak it in now. I took a good look at everything going on around me: other runners for as far as I could see, all bouncing along as strangers cheered us on from the sidewalk. They were holding up signs saying things like, "You got this!" "Go Lucy," and several humorous, hurtful ones like, "If it was easy, it would be your mother" (all actual signs people hold up at marathons).

Kids in the crowd also held out their hands hoping for high fives, and I obliged several. I stopped doing this after I imagined I was losing momentum with each high five, like a spinning carnival wheel with pegs on it, slowing as it passes a clicker hitting each peg. (If you need a reference, see the "Showcase Showdown" on *The Price Is Right*.) There was also music, some live, some blasting out of boom boxes, and there was even an Elvis impersonator. Elvis being alive or Elvis being a fan of marathons: Which would be more surprising? This theoretical question filled my mind as I ran the next few blocks. Thank you, fake Elvis, for that very real distraction.

MILE 3

As mentioned before, I always found the first three miles of any run were the most difficult. It just takes my body and legs that long to wake up and settle into a rhythm (although the way I run, there really is no trace of any rhythm—just like jazz!). Even though I was excited and full of adrenaline, the marathon was no different. It took me until about the third mile before I calmed down and settled in.

The three-mile marker is also where I first came across an aid station. There would be one every mile from this point on, each of them stocked with pre-filled cups of Gatorade and water, handed to runners by generous and selfless volunteers. I tried to say "thank you" every time I took a cup from them, but I know my expressions of gratitude were lost in a cacophony of wheezes and death gurgles as the race went on. If, by chance, you are reading this and you were one of those volunteers, let me give you a very sincere, heartfelt death gurgle.

MILE 4

Did someone ask about my nipples? Well, they were doing fine, because I had greased them up that morning with the dedication of a NASCAR pit crew. Even if I hadn't, human kindness was looking out for my fellow participants and me. Among the crowd, strangers were handing runners Popsicle sticks with Vaseline on them, to smear on their nipples. I had heard what a life-affirming thing a marathon can be, but I wasn't ready for that moment of universal connectedness when a complete stranger felt concern for my nipples. Hoping to settle the debt, I plan one day to walk around Brooklyn with an industrial-size drum of Vaseline, asking passersby about their nipples. I'm sure nothing bad will come from this.

MILE 5

I had been running for about fifty minutes, and I was feeling fine. I knew it had been about fifty minutes because even though I didn't join a pace team, I was constantly looking at my GPS watch, watching my pace, and still moving at roughly ten minutes per mile. Based on my carefully marked pace bracelet, I saw it was time for my first gel. I reached into my shorts, took out a silver pouch full of lukewarm vanilla something, and ingested it. It was, in a word, horrible. It was, in two words, really horrible.

MILE 6

Now about an hour in, I was growing a little weary. I needed a shot of motivation/tequila/encouragement. The signs fans were holding up had lost their effectiveness, even the ones reading "Worst Parade Ever!" and "Kenyans are drinking the beer—run faster!" Luckily I then passed a runner who inspired me.

To really break it down, I was 3 percent inspired because I actually passed someone and 97 percent inspired because the runner was a member of the Achilles Track Club. This is a running club that helps train and support runners at all levels, including runners like this one, who was physically disabled.

That's right, this gentleman was physically disabled and was running a marathon. He had the help of two guides, but still, he was running the same marathon I was, undeterred by his limitations. Seeing him go, I felt a little guilty for the twelve thousand complaints I had muttered so far (roughly one per step). I was "healthy," so what did I have to complain about?

I wanted to wish this guy well and thank him for reminding me to be grateful instead of grumpy, all without sounding patronizing. In the end, I just croaked out a weak "Go Achilles" and continued on. I hope that gave this true athlete a fraction of the boost he gave me. We went our separate ways, both swallowed up by the crowd, and in his honor, I didn't complain at all for the next three blocks (give or take two blocks).

MILE 9

Wait, what happened to miles seven and eight? Now is the time for me to tell you—I'm not going to describe every mile (I'm lazy, remember?). Here at mile nine, I was still moving, still in Brooklyn, and still feeling pretty good. We had been in Brooklyn for a while now, and I was starting to get a little disappointed. My expectations for what I would see in Brooklyn were based in complete ignorance—that's how most Americans travel, right? I had heard that Brooklyn was full of hipsters. The whole borough was supposed to be the cool, bohemian part of New York City, yet I hadn't seen even one hipster. I felt like I had booked a cruise and still hadn't seen a drop of water.

But then, the environs started to change. The crowds thinned, and suddenly people on the street were indeed wearing beards and hats! Unfortunately these weren't hipsters—instead, we were running through the part of Brooklyn populated by Orthodox Jews. This was completely unexpected. Even more unexpected was the reality that at that moment, I just may have been the hippest guy in Brooklyn.

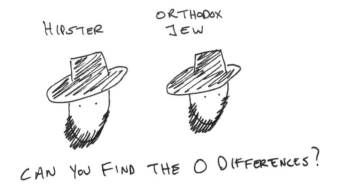

I'd like to take a minute to give a special shout-out to the Orthodox Jews for one thing: Everywhere else on the course, people lined the streets, held signs, cheered, high-fived, handed out Vaseline for sore nipples, etc., but the Orthodox Jews showed zero interest in the marathon. They treated the whole thing with the same enthusiasm they might have for a bacon giveaway. I'm Jewish; didn't that merit a little support? Didn't they know that one of their own, the former I. L. Peretz School sprint champion, was stumbling past?

Sundays are workdays in the Orthodox community, and that's why they hurried about, virtually ignoring the fifty thousand people running past in fluorescent, heavily logoed outfits. Every now and then, one of them may have looked over for a second at the parade of sweat going by, but without a doubt, this was the quietest, least energized part of the race. Future runners, if noise, bands, cheering, thumping of feet, and excitement bother you, you have this silent oasis to look forward to. You can run in peace, maybe meditate, read a book, catch up on emails, whatever.

MILE 11

Finally, hipsters! The Williamsburg section of Brooklyn was exactly what I was hoping for: cool, vibrant, and full of signs announcing the manufacture of artisanal cheese, pickles, and chocolate. My pace was still good—right around ten minutes a mile. My legs felt OK. I was hydrating and had almost gotten the taste of the energy gel out of my mouth. Why couldn't one of these hipsters come up with an artisanal energy gel? Why? Why!!!

MILE 13

This point in the race was notable for a couple reasons. One, I was nearing the halfway point, and two, I was about to enter Queens. I didn't know what to expect in Queens, and let me tell you, it lived up to those expectations.

Physically, I was still on pace, still feeling good. It was way too early to think I may make it to the end without dying, but I'd almost made it halfway without dying, so that was encouraging.

I had been running for just over two hours. I realized I wouldn't be running the first sub-two-hour marathon. Everyone said there would be some mental setbacks during the race—this must have been what they were talking about.

This was also when I had to come to terms with the fact that I wasn't going to win this thing. The elite athletes were already at the finish line. I had lost lots of other stuff (hockey games, baby teeth, consciousness), but I had never lost something this big before. I tried to take some satisfaction in the fact that I was taking my losing to the next level. This was an epic loss, and I was nailing it. This must be the same weak rationalizing Mitt Romney did after the 2012 presidential election.

MILE 16

This mile features the Queensboro Bridge (a.k.a. the "Queensboro Hill," at least to my legs). This bridge is unique because no spectators are allowed on it. Consequently it's quiet, even quieter than the Orthodox Jewish section of Brooklyn. The difference is, there is a sense of excitement on the bridge, because runners know that when the bridge ends, Manhattan begins. Not just Manhattan, but First Avenue, where traditionally the loudest crowds of the race gather.

I knew none of this, but I learned it as I chatted with a guy next to me while we headed down the bridge. My new friend told me that this was his favorite part of the race, saying that when you come off the bridge and out of the quiet, you are launched into a tornado of cheers. He described it as being "like running onto the field at the Super Bowl." Worried about being sued by the NFL for copyright infringement, I said, "Don't you mean, 'Like running onto the field at the 'big game?'" He gave me a disturbed look and gently increased his pace, leaving me alone. Friendship over.

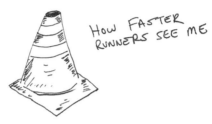

HOW FASTER RUNNERS SEE ME

When I came off the bridge, as promised, the crowd was waiting. They were loud, and supportive, and it was awesome. I needed that little boost, because at this point in the race, I was starting to feel some pain. The bridges were taking their toll. Not actual tolls—that would have made the race expensive and really hurt people's times, but my legs were starting to weaken.

I did something here, at the sixteen-mile mark, that in retrospect I was very proud of. I took two aspirins. I know that doesn't seem like a huge accomplishment, but at that time, at that place, it was. Those aspirin shut my legs up for the next couple hours and allowed me to focus instead on all the other parts of my body that were screaming. My legs kept moving, and so did I—into Manhattan.

MILE 18

Harlem. Another area I had ignorant preconceptions about, and again they were all proven wrong. The people of Harlem lined the street and were excited and supportive as I trudged onward. I needed that support, because I was now really starting to struggle: aches, exhaustion, sore feet, and a sapped will. I thought about death here, writing and rewriting my obituary as I ran. I kept trying to work in the phrase "Canada's Golden Gift to Eternity," but I worried it may come off as a little conceited.

Very few people actually die running a marathon; only about one in every one hundred thousand. There were fifty thousand people in my race, which meant that on that day, half a person would die. I realized that half person was my lower half. My legs. The legs of Canada's Golden Gift to Eternity.

MILE 19

I kept pushing forward, head down, watching my body submit to this repeated pounding. This was unnatural. There had to be a better way to do this. By better, of course, I mean lazier. I could have trained harder, or improved my running form, but I also could have planned a shortcut. I started to think about cheating. Both my legs and morals were weakening.

I'm not the first person to think about cheating to get through a marathon—several others have done it before me, and according the *New York Times*, roughly 0.01 percent of runners each year skirt the rules. Cheating was yet another facet of running I had no chance of being first at, not even in my age group.

There is a multitude of ways people have cheated, but they generally fall into one of two categories:

1) Cutting the course. This is particularly enticing since the marathon goes through Manhattan twice, and there is an easy rerouting that takes off nine miles. The problem with this is that there are time strips all along the course, and each one registers your progress and pace. Missing several of them highlights your cheating, not to mention the sudden change in your overall pace (having lost nine miles).

People have also been busted by their appearance in the many amateur and professional photographs taken along the way.

One infamous course cutter was Rosie Ruiz, who "won" the 1980 Boston Marathon by leaving the race, riding the subway, and rejoining the race later on. I admire her not only for her nerve, but also for avoiding even walking to cut the course. That is laziness I can only aspire to.

2) Bib-swapping. This is getting someone faster to run in your place, or running half the race and then handing your bib to someone fresh to finish it. The benefit of this is posting a better time in your name and even possibly qualifying to run in the Boston Marathon.

Neither method was for me. I knew I couldn't cheat. I didn't have the nerve, the deviousness, or the subway pass. I kept puffing along, just like a sucker.

MILE 20

Sweaty, tired, and tired of being sweaty, I was now entering the last borough before turning back into Manhattan: the Bronx, another place I had never been. I was also about to run farther than I ever had before.

While training, the longest prescribed run is set at twenty miles. The wisdom behind this approach is that twenty miles is enough to test your endurance without risking the injury you may get by running the full marathon distance. No, you want to save that injury for the actual race instead.

Anyway, here I was about to break my old record, to be on the other side, to cross a new frontier. The closest previous experience I had to this was the day I decided to check out the channels higher than three hundred on my TV. What an adventure! I saw Bollywood films, Chinese news stories, home shopping! I made it through that; I should be able to make it through this. I continued on.

Mile 20 is also infamous because it's when runners often "hit the wall" or "bonk." To avoid this, I kept eating (slurping? chewing? tolerating?) energy gels and drinking Gatorade. Luckily for me, it worked. My body had enough calories to avoid disaster and keep me puttering along.

In case you are curious, I didn't see anybody else bonk, either. I saw people who had pulled over and were walking. I saw runners stretching. I saw my fair share of public urination. (Maybe even more than my share, but I am more than happy to return the excess portion to the rightful owner.) Most people, like me, just bore down and kept moving.

The course headed back into Manhattan now, for the home stretch. Unfortunately, the route was along Fifth Avenue. This is an expensive neighborhood, and like most expensive neighborhoods, getting there demands an uphill climb. Unlike some expensive neighborhoods, however, there was no way a huge inheritance could help you avoid this hill, unless you inherited antigravity boots that made topography irrelevant.

I know, the story of someone inheriting antigravity boots and moving into a New York high-rise sounds way more interesting than this one about me running a marathon. Right now, you're probably thinking about buying a book on that, but look how close I am to the end of the race! Look how close you are to the end of this book! Hang in there! You can do this—you *can* make it to the end (even if I don't). I believe in you!

MILE 23

Still climbing this subtle hill, we were on what's called Museum Mile. It's called that because it includes world-famous museums like the Guggenheim and the National Academy Museum. I'm not usually someone who would choose to go into a museum, but right then, I would have in a second, just to sit down. It made me think the whole marathon was a long con organized by the museums, to make people want to go inside. Thoughts like this were proof my brain was as tired as my body, both on the edge of giving up.

MILE 24

I knew we were getting close to the finish when the course turned into Central Park. It was spectacularly beautiful; an exhibition of fall colors (far better, I'm sure, than whatever garbage exhibitions were hanging on the walls of the museums I just ran by).

I was tired, I was excited, but here, right as we got into the park, something happened I won't soon forget.

You may recall earlier when I mentioned that people wrote their names on their shirts to elicit encouragement from the crowd. Well, since we are recalling, also recall that I had chosen to wear the shirt with the logo of Shoe4Africa, the charity I was running for. This was why, when I was slogging through Central Park, every part of me aching, my spirit drained, a very well-meaning woman leaned out of the crowd, and seeing me, a white, Jewish-Canadian guy, got in my face and screamed, "You got this, Africa!"

The marathon may be a once in a lifetime experience; however, it's not impossible that I could run another one. But even if I run a thousand, this will certainly never happen to me again.

MILE 25

I could almost smell the finish. I say "almost" because this is New York, which mostly smells like counterfeit purses and street hot dogs (both made out of the same material!). Still, the crowd was louder as we burst out of Central Park and began running next to it, along Central Park South. We were heading toward Columbus Circle, where we would make the final turn toward the finish line.

I was in pain, mentally and physically exhausted, but I knew I just had to push through this final (uphill, of course!) stretch. I reached into the tank for that last little bit of gas, but there was none. OK, no reason to panic. I told myself, "I can do this without gas." I just needed to think of my body as an electric car. As I tried again to pick up my quickly slowing pace, it became clear that if I was an electric car, I hadn't been plugged in overnight, and someone had left that little light above the rearview mirror on. I was spent; my battery drained. It was a struggle to even keep close to my ten-minute pace. I grimaced and put my head down, willing myself to just keep going forward, the pain making my legs tremble.

When I next lifted my head, I saw Columbus Circle straight ahead. I was almost done. Things started happening fast. The pack around me, sensing the finish, surged forward, and surprisingly, I surged with them. Part of this surge had to do with the fact that this part of the course was downhill. Yes, *down* a hill. Up until then, I didn't even know hills in New York could go down. This one did, and it couldn't have come at a better time.

I forced myself forward, passing the giant banners that detailed how far the finish was. 1000 meters . . . 800 meters . . . 600 meters . . . The crowd noise grew louder and louder, and finally, I realized I was going to do this. I was going to make it!

Wanting to finish with a bit of a final push, I scraped together every carb I could find in my body. I lifted heavy legs, swung sore hips, and . . . I did it!

I, a lazy pyramid of lard, had somehow just run the New York City Marathon.

COME TO TERMS WITH YOUR FAILURE

26

> "Everything you ever wanted to know about yourself, you can learn in 26.2 miles."
> —LORI CULNANE, AMATEUR MARATHONER
>
> (Several psychologists are suing Ms. Culnane for ruining their business.)

Crossing the time strip, cruising under the huge FINISH banner, my first reward was the right to stop running. Easier said than done. As exhausted as I was, my legs had been pounding out ten-minute miles all morning, and now that their shift was over, it took a couple seconds to settle into a walk. When I did, it wasn't a pretty walk. I looked like a marionette whose puppeteer was being electrocuted.

With that hobbled gait, I moved toward a waiting sea of volunteers. The first one draped a finisher medal over my neck. The second one wrapped me in a shawl that was as hideously orange as it was warm. It felt good against my sweat-soaked body just now noticing the fifty-degree weather. I think someone took my picture, but at that moment, someone could have taken my kidney and I wouldn't have noticed.

I looked at my watch. My mile splits weren't spectacular, but they were consistent; ten-minute miles until right at the end when I fell off a little. Still, all of those individual miles added up to a total time of:

4:26:03

I had beaten four and a half hours! I had beaten Oprah!

That's right, Oprah, a guy you've never met, and don't even know exists, beat your marathon time! Next I'm gonna get my own talk show, magazine, and become best friends with Gayle King, whoever that is. Vindicated and victorious, I smiled.

The purists in the running community would suggest I had nothing to smile about. If you recall, they claim that anything over four hours isn't a good time and further suggest that slow runners like me aren't really runners at all. In their eyes, clocking in at over four hours diminishes the magnitude of "finishing a marathon." This faction of the running community is even angry with Oprah for suggesting to the masses that running a "slow" marathon is OK. To be fair, I've considered this purist argument, and after long thought, have constructed the following response: The short version is "screw you." A longer version follows:

This elitist view of running suggests that no one should ever do anything unless they can do it at the highest level. Do these "purists" believe that they should be allowed to run their three-hour marathons when elite athletes are running them in two hours? Who is setting the bar where "acceptable" lives? What about other sports? Should someone be able to play golf even if they can't break one hundred? What about someone slowly doing charity work—don't even bother? Is someone trying to get sober in six months wasting his or her time when someone else can do it in five months? Should I be allowed to list these shoddy examples when someone else (anyone else) could provide better ones?

To any so-called purist out there, I challenge you to stand at the finish line of a marathon and tell these slow runners their marathon doesn't count. I contend that it actually may "count" more than yours does. These are people like me, who never thought they could run a marathon, and then they did. They didn't just do something they had done a little better than the last time; they did something they thought was impossible.

The finish line I was standing at in Central Park was an impressive display of raw emotion. There were tears, hugs, smiles—a collage of pride, accomplishment, relief, anguish, and joy.

In my job, there is the tendency to mute emotions, to try to make a joke of anything and everything, and therefore sometimes sincerity suffers. As a result of the job, or some inner flaw, I am unfortunately a little jaded—even more jaded than a Chinese lady's bracelet! See? I couldn't even resist adding a joke here (although it may not qualify as a joke; it's in the lab now being analyzed).

Regardless, even I, an emotionless husk imitating an actual person, found myself caught up in the positive and pure emotions of the finishers around me. I realized I was proud of all these strangers, and then, even more shocking, I realized I was proud of myself. I too had just finished a marathon!

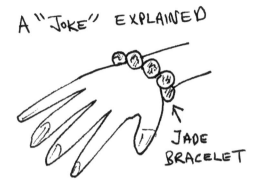

A "JOKE" EXPLAINED

JADE BRACELET

I've had other accomplishments in my life, and I can look back on them fondly. In most cases, however, being truthful, a lot of these accomplishments were a team effort, relying upon luck, coincidence, and a myriad of other factors, including talent and persistence. Running a marathon was different. It was a clearly defined goal that could be achieved only by me training and committing to it. No help from anyone. Knowing that, knowing I did this on my own, made the accomplishment so much more. It made it a victory.

My high was reinforced even more as I talked to my family and heard my wife and daughters gush congratulations, impressed that I had done what I set out to do so many months before. As I staggered back to my hotel, entirely inconspicuous in my bright orange blanket, almost every New Yorker I passed—also normally jaded and cynical—said "congratulations."

Back at the hotel, I read several texts and emails congratulating me. The next day, as I limped around the city, I saw several other runners wearing their medals around their necks. I didn't have mine on, worried I wouldn't be able to support the additional weight on my savaged legs, but people saw my tender, measured gait and knew to offer me congratulations as well. What neither I nor any of my medal-wearing comrades ever heard was, "What was your time?"

People even wore their medals on my flight home and were congratulated by passengers and crew alike. Knowing I was part of this, I was so buoyant, I barely noticed the two-hour flight delay. When I finally walked/stumbled into work, I got a standing ovation from my colleagues who spend their days sitting. Normally, they probably wouldn't even stand for a fire; instead they'd just roll their chairs out into the parking lot and make sure someone rescued the snacks. Of course, once the applause stopped, my coworkers asked if I had thrown up on myself during the race. Beaming with pride, chest puffed out, I told them no, I had not.

The point is, the excitement everyone had for what my fellow runners and I had done was as exciting as the race itself. It reinforced the accomplishment without ever once trying to qualify it as "good" or "less than good." So purists—up yours.

I know this book is called *How to Lose a Marathon*, but like the rest of the book, the title is questionable. There's no way to lose a marathon; every single person who runs one wins. I know this creates a lot of confusion about how to divide the prize money given to the first place finisher, but let the organizers figure that out.

Even though I finished deep in the middle of a fifty thousand runner field, even though the medal they put around my neck was the same medal they also put around fifty thousand other necks, and even though the newspaper the next day did not mention my personal victory or my demolition of Oprah, all of those non-events don't mean I didn't win, because I did. I won the New York City Marathon. As Maya Angelou said, and many bad lawyers have re-quoted, "Facts can obscure the truth."

WORLD'S SHORTEST EPILOGUE

26.2

> "Running is the greatest metaphor for life, because you get out of it what you put into it."
> —OPRAH WINFREY, MY BILLIONAIRE NEMESIS
>
> (Ignore this. Why listen to her when you can listen to the guy who beat her time by two minutes?)

2014 CHICAGO MARATHON, 4:44:01

I ran another marathon less than a year later. I felt ready for it. I was older, wiser, and also about eighteen minutes slower. It's worth noting that even though my time was worse, in New York I finished in 26,782nd place, and in Chicago, I placed 24,862nd, an improvement of 1,920 places. Apparently, with each race, I get about two thousand spots closer to first place. At this pace, I'm only thirteen marathons away from actually winning one. All I need to do is keep training, keep improving, and keep ignoring the logic or reality of this ridiculous thesis.

THE END

THE MOST BORING APPENDIX EVER WRITTEN

I think I crushed this. Here, I have written the most boring collection of text ever known to man. Apologies to every other author who has tried to craft pages so boring that anyone with working arms or eyes would immediately flip past, but I think I've nailed it with this dry relisting of the details of my training runs. If you are drawn to masochism, a great/horrible way to further crank up the boring here is to have someone read this to you in a monotone voice, maybe while a faucet drips slowly in the background.

NOTE: These are not the runs from when I started, but rather the runs that were part of my marathon training program. The program is sixteen weeks long, so working backward with the marathon in November, I started to train in July. It's telling that I started in the hottest month of the year. It confirms that I am both an idiot and a glutton for punishment. Interestingly, I'm also a glutton for ribs, ice cream, and a lot of other things.

DATE	DISTANCE	PACE
07/15	4.03 miles	10:50 min/mile

This was listed in the program as four miles at an "easy pace." You can see I embraced the idea of an easy pace.

| 07/17 | 4.13 miles | 10:44 min/mile |
| 07/19 | — | — |

The 19th was supposed to be another 4-mile run, but I skipped it. I don't remember why, but if I have to make up an excuse now, let's say I was giving blood to puppies in a shelter. That sounds like the kind of thing I might lie about doing.

TIP: I didn't do every run in the schedule. But, even here, missing one so early, I decided not to get too hung up about it and didn't try to make up the run because it would have thrown me off. I just jumped back on track with the next run. This decision took away some of the stress of not following things exactly. So if you happen to miss a run here and there, don't worry about it. Spend that non-running time rationalizing, like I did.

| 07/21 | 8.00 miles | 10:39 min/mile |

Yup, eight miles. But I let it take as long as it took, and it took about an hour and a half.

| 07/23 | 4.39 miles | 10:54 min/mile |
| 07/24 | 6.59 miles | 09:41 min/mile |

I wish I could explain why my pace was faster here. Was it wind? Downhill? I attribute it to computer error (same reason I assume I was ever accepted into college).

DATE	DISTANCE	PACE
07/26	4.02 miles	10:54 min/mile
07/28	14.40 miles	09:54 min/mile
07/30	1.53 miles	10:23 min/mile
07/30	0.42 miles	09:44 min/mile
07/30	4.03 miles	10:00 min/mile

OK, I know I have three entries for the same date. What happened was my finger kept slipping and stopping the app, and I would have to restart it again. It took me two tries to figure out how not to let my finger slip. We can focus on the two failures, or we can celebrate the incredible victory of figuring it out. I choose the latter, but that's just my sunny, positive disposition coming out.

07/31	11.00 miles	10:43 min/mile
08/05	5.01 miles	10:45 min/mile
08/07	6.00 miles	09:34 min/mile

By now, you've noticed that sometimes the distances don't stop exactly on a mile. This is because sometimes they are interval/tempo/other runs based on time rather than distance. Sometimes I would run a little past the stopping point to get to my car, and sometimes I was just too exhausted to push the "stop" button.

08/09	4.29 miles	10:29 min/mile
08/10	12.01 miles	10:21 min/mile
08/12	4.27 miles	11:08 min/mile

A pace of eleven minutes? I wish I could tell you why that happened, but I have no idea. I think the safest thing to assume is that the app was broken that day and then worked perfectly on my next run when I had a scorching 9:33 pace.

08/14	7.05 miles	09:33 min/mile
08/17	13.11 miles	10:31 min/mile
08/19	4.69 miles	10:43 min/mile
08/21	3.98 miles	09:45 min/mile
08/21	1.03 miles	10:08 min/mile

Yes, I know, two entries. Finger slipped again. I need a better phone (or a better finger).

DATE	DISTANCE	PACE
08/23	5.01 miles	08:34 min/mile
08/24	8.10 miles	09:52 min/mile
08/27	6.08 miles	09:31 min/mile
08/31	12.00 miles	10:42 min/mile
09/02	6.00 miles	09:55 min/mile
09/04	6.06 miles	09:38 min/mile
09/06	5.00 miles	09:45 min/mile
09/07	15.01 miles	10:29 min/mile
09/09	5.79 miles	10:22 min/mile
09/11	7.04 miles	10:10 min/mile
09/13	5.03 miles	09:27 min/mile
09/14	18.02 miles	10:13 min/mile
09/15	1.05 miles	10:58 min/mile
09/16	4.74 miles	10:38 min/mile

Not sure what happened here. I either ran three consecutive days, or I ran so slow that it took me three days to finish. Most likely, I screwed something up again.

09/20	7.04 miles	09:41 min/mile
09/24	5.08 miles	09:26 min/mile
09/27	7.59 miles	09:10 min/mile

A 9:10 pace? 9:10? I started to suspect that I was taking steroids.

09/29	20.04 miles	09:49 min/mile

This was the longest run of the entire training program. Training wisdom is you don't run the full marathon distance until the race itself, but by running twenty miles, you prove to yourself and your body you can get at least that far. I barely made it through these twenty miles, leaving both me and my body worried.

10/01	5.11 miles	10:18 min/mile
10/03	8.24 miles	09:44 min/mile
10/04	6.02 miles	09:51 min/mile
10/06	14.02 miles	09:36 min/mile

DATE	DISTANCE	PACE
10/08	7.21 miles	09:17 min/mile
10/11	4.02 miles	09:31 min/mile
10/12	17.61 miles	10:18 min/mile
10/13	8.62 miles	09:30 min/mile
10/15	4.02 miles	09:59 min/mile
10/17	6.02 miles	09:26 min/mile
10/18	6.01 miles	09:00 min/mile
10/20	13.12 miles	09:21 min/mile

This was supposed to be a ten-mile run, but for some reason I added miles here to run a half marathon. It wasn't in the training plan, but I did it. I'm a rebel.

10/22	5.05 miles	10:03 min/mile

This was the start of the taper.

10/23	5.33 miles	10:04 min/mile
10/25	5.02 miles	09:54 min/mile
10/26	6.01 miles	09:37 min/mile
10/29	3.87 miles	11:11 min/mile
10/31	3.00 miles	10:20 min/mile
11/02	2.00 miles	10:00 min/mile

This was my team shakeout run.

11/03	THE MARATHON	(GULP)

THINGS I'VE LOST

KEYS

MITTENS

CONSCIOUSNESS

A MARATHON

GLOSSARY

Speak runner like a native! Here's every additional running term you would ever need, or at least the ones I know (or at least the ones I think I know).

BQ: I see this acronym and think it is only one "B" away from BBQ, or barbecue, which I understand all too well. Runners see this and know it stands for Boston Qualifying time, which I barely understand at all.

CROSS-TRAINING: Adding sports other than running to your training regimen to improve overall fitness and strength. If you are looking to decrease fitness and strength, eat nachos while watching a documentary on cross-training.

DNS/DNF: DNS (did not start) or DNF (did not finish) is what will appear in the race results if a runner doesn't start or finish a race. DMZ means they have somehow found their way into the demilitarized zone between North and South Korea. If that happens to you, I suggest heading to South Korea, but obviously the choice is up to you.

ELEVATION CHART: Most races provide these beforehand to participants. They show the changes in elevation by mile along the course so you can see where the hills are and be mentally and physically prepared. Some races try to entice entrants with the promise of a "net overall downhill" (which is also how many people have described my career).

PB: Personal best. A PB is beating yourself, running faster than you ever have before. It's what people concentrate on once they've come to terms with the fact that they probably aren't going to win the race. To get a PB, just run your first race, and you will instantly achieve one! When bragging about it, if someone asks, "What was your old time?" be ready to change the subject—maybe by mentioning how long potters wait before glazing an urn they've made (three days).

PR: Personal record. An alternate term for a PB. Before I started running, I thought PR stood for "public relations" or Puerto Rico, but like with so many things, I was wrong. Before you pity me for my stupidity, think about the poor people who work in PR for the Puerto Rico Marathon. They deserve your pity more than I do.

SINGLETS: This is the odd, confusing term for the sleeveless tank tops some runners wear. Don't ask a runner why that's the name; they don't know. No one knows. It's a mystery, like if you should tip the server after eating at a restaurant buffet.

TRAIL RUNNING: Running on a trail, as opposed to a smooth path or road. Trails provide nice variation in scenery, elevation, and which muscles you use because of the uneven surfaces. Watch out for rocks, roots, and, well, uneven surfaces.

TRIATHLON: Before I started running, I was sure this was just a poorly spelled ad for the luggage maker Athalon. It isn't. A triathlon is a race that combines swimming, biking, and running. The most famous triathlons are the Ironman series, which are held all over the world and include a 2.4-mile swim, a 112-mile bike ride, and then a full marathon, in that order. Typing that last sentence is as close as I will ever get to participating in one.

ULTRAMARATHON: These are races for people not satisfied with running just 26.2 miles. Ultramarathon races can be 50K, 100K, 50 miles, or 100 miles. The best known of these is the South African Comrades Marathon, which has been held since 1921. The race promotes itself as a "symbol of camaraderie, selfless-ness, dedication, perseverance, and *ubuntu*." For a definition of *ubuntu*, read my never-to-be-written English to Zulu dictionary.

FOR YOUR LISTENING DISTRACTION

A list of some running-related books I have enjoyed (in no particular order—that would have taken work).

NOTE: Without exception, I consumed all of these as audiobooks, listening as I ran instead of actually reading them. I don't know if listening to a book still counts as reading it. The US Supreme Court is expected to rule on this next year.

Born to Run by Christopher McDougall: A great read, full of information and inspiration, and the reason I started this whole running thing.

Shoe Dog by Phil Knight: Not so much a book about running as a book about starting Nike, the biggest brand in athletic shoes. Regardless, the perseverance behind launching what is now a behemoth is inspiring on its own.

A Race Like No Other by Liz Robbins: An in-depth look at the New York City Marathon, told through several interwoven personal stories.

Running for My Life by Lopez Lomong: The story of a Sudanese Lost Boy who becomes a member of the US Olympic team.

My Best Race edited by Chris Cooper: Short essays from runners of all levels.

Running with the Kenyans by Adharanand Finn: Part travelogue, part memoir, Mr. Finn lived in Kenya and tried to understand why Kenya keeps producing some of the world's best runners.

What I Talk About When I Talk About Running by Haruki Murakami: A cerebral (i.e., too smart for me) and introspective look at running and life.

Triumph by Jeremy Schaap: The story of African-American runner Jesse Owens at the 1936 Berlin Olympics in Nazi Germany.

The Long Run by Matt Long and Charles Butler: The story of a New York firefighter and triathlete who suffered and then came back from a devastating accident.

The Perfect Mile by Neal Bascomb: A captivating retelling of the race to run the first four-minute mile.

The Boys in the Boat by Daniel James Brown: Not a running book at all. It's about rowing. But it's also awesome and inspirational.

THANKS

I've never written a book before. Some would say I still haven't.

Whatever I did or didn't do I couldn't have done or not done without the help of many, and now, like it or not, those people are about to be acknowledged! (Lamest threat ever uttered?)

First, of course, is my lovely and supportive wife Sandi, and our daughters Rachel and Samara. Yes, I'm intentionally excluding our dog Coco, who frankly was not helpful or supportive.

Mega-thanks are due to my editor Samantha Weiner. From our first phone call to the last line of the last draft, she guided, suggested, improved, and made the whole process easy and enjoyable. I can only hope we are still speaking as you read this.

A (written) standing ovation for designer Devin Grosz. He applied his magic to every illustration (a word never misused more than for my lousy stick drawings) and facet of the layout to make this book look as good as it does.

A shout out to Rob LaZebnik and John Frink, two of my frequent *Simpsons* collaborators, who both gave me helpful notes and lied to tell me this was "good." I thank them for their assistance and dishonesty.

Thank you also to my agents Sasha Raskin and Mickey Berman at UTA. If I didn't thank them, I fear reprisals, both professional and physical. I'm joking of course. (No I'm not.)

And since I still have room on the page, let me thank all of my family, Runkeeper, Shoe4Africa, everyone involved with the New York City Marathon, everyone at *The Simpsons*, and whoever is immediately to your left as you read this. If you don't know them, introduce yourself and tell them they've been acknowledged. If this somehow frightens them and they use pepper spray on you:

1. Don't touch the affected area.

2. Blink rapidly to cause your eyes to tear up.

3. Wash your skin with hand soap, shampoo, or even dish soap and rinse with water.

4. Use a "no tears" baby shampoo to help rinse your eye area.

The above is free advice and a little teaser from my next book, *So You've Been Pepper Sprayed*. It will be sold at leading riots everywhere.